soul shaper

Becoming the Person God Wants You to Be

KEITH DRURY

wesleyan
publishing
house

Indianapolis, Indiana

To my wife, Sharon, who practices these disciplines
better than anyone I know.

contents

preface

You have a soul. In some ways, you are a soul. You are more than flesh, bones, and electrical signals between your brain's synapses. There is—inside you—a real you. It is gone when your body dies. Christians call this a soul (or sometimes the heart). Your soul is more than material "stuff," but it affects what you do in the flesh. The shape of your soul inclines you to sin or obedience, revenge or forgiveness, pride or humility. But the good news is your soul can change!

This book is about the spiritual disciplines, but they are not soul shapers. There is only one soul shaper and it is not a spiritual discipline; God is the soul shaper. Spiritual disciplines are not rungs on a ladder leading you to godliness. Treating the disciplines like that is a tower of Babel. Jesus himself struck down the self-righteous clambering for godliness—the Pharisees. God is the soul shaper, not these practices.

So if God is the shaper of your soul, what is left for you to do? Should you relax in your sin and wait for God to change you in his own good time? No, because you have a part in God's work, even though he is the one who does it. You can hinder God's shaping work with denial and resistance, but you can help God with surrender and obedience.

This is where the spiritual disciplines come in. Or we might call them the "means of grace." These disciplines are practices we can do that put us in the channel of God's changing grace. In solitude, confession, restitution, or peacemaking, God chooses to change us. The disciplines are channels of God's grace to get under.

PART 1
disciplines of abstinence

In the disciplines of abstinence, we abstain from things that can distance us from God. These disciplines become a means of grace, a channel through which God can change us as we clear away the clutter that blocks the path to him.

Our world is a busy one, and we often feel guilty that we aren't adding enough good things to our lives to make us more like Christ. But we must *subtract* from our lives before we can add to them. That makes the disciplines of abstinence the best place for busy people to begin their journey to Christlikeness. These practices create space in which we can hear God. They also create space in which we can do things—the disciplines of action, which we'll talk about later.

In fasting, we abstain from food. In silence, we abstain from noise and from speaking. In solitude, we abstain from companionship and crowds. In simplicity, we abstain from an abundance of material things. In rest, we abstain from the frantic pace of work. In secrecy, we abstain from taking credit for the good things we do. The abstinence itself does not make us better people. But by abstaining from these things for a time, we get a better sense of God's presence which changes us.

1. fasting *temperance prudence*

So when you give to the needy . . .
And when you pray . . . When you fast . . .

—Matthew 6:2, 5, 16

something essential

Fasting is abstaining from food for a time in order to gain
mastery of the physical realm and open us up to the spiritual.
Christians have consistently practiced fasting through the ages
as a way to get closer to God. But even before there were
Christians, the Jewish people fasted twice a week and at other
set times throughout the year. In fact, people of most religions
fast. The idea that we can reach out to God in this way seems to
be built into the very nature of human beings. Jesus simply assumed
that his followers would fast and gave instructions on how to do it
(see Matt. 6:16). He did not say, "*If* you fast, do not look somber as
the hypocrites do." He said, "*When* you fast . . ." In those days, it
was assumed that people practiced this discipline, and ever since
then, it has been assumed that fasting is an important part of the

Christian lifestyle. Until recently, that is. Only in contemporary times have Christians concluded that praying and reading the Bible are required but fasting is optional. Now, instead of fasting, we diet.

fasting and dieting

Diets help us lose weight, but dieting is not fasting. When dieting, we abstain from food (or fats or carbohydrates or whatever the most recent fad is) in order to lose the extra fat we have gained from eating too much. Diets are about losing weight so we can look nicer, feel better, and live longer; fasting is about growing closer to God. When we fast, we deny our appetites and take control of our flesh. In the process, our spirits gain mastery of other fleshly desires. Dieting can be a good thing, but fasting is better. Fasting provides some of the same benefits as dieting but adds a closer walk with God. Dieting is a fifty-billion-dollar-a-year business in North America. There is no money in fasting, but the benefits are priceless. What fasting promises is a nearness to the heart of God.

our obsession with food

We diet because we are fat—or think we are. For those of us living in a land of abundance, the concern is not where to find our next bite, but how to remedy eating *too many* bites. Our culture is obsessed with food. Eating is a sensory—even sensuous—experience for us. We crave the fleshly satisfaction food brings to the eye or tongue; we even enjoy the feeling of being stuffed after a Thanksgiving dinner. The way food looks, tastes, smells, and feels is far more important to us than its nutritional value.

We use food mostly for pleasure. Most preachers and church members alike overlook this near gluttony or dismiss it jokingly. The church usually tries to restrain us from going overboard in gratifying other sensory pleasures, but it seems to celebrate excessive eating. The world is worse. Flip through a women's magazine sometime and count the pictures of food. Men, too, struggle with the addiction to eating as a sensory pleasure. John Wesley wrote of this danger more than two hundred years ago. Early church fathers such as Clement wrote extensively on it. Today, few people take these matters seriously for we have come to accept and approve of this sensuousness. All cultures have evils they pronounce as good. In North America, overeating is one of them.

putting food in its place

Fasting is a way to put food in its place. It is a means of liberating ourselves—even if only for a short time—from food's dominating control. When we conclude a time of fasting, we come away with a different perspective; we see food as fuel for living more than as a sensory pleasure. Isn't that God's perspective on food? Didn't he intend for food to primarily be fuel for the body and only secondarily as a source of sensuous satisfaction? It is not that we cannot or should not enjoy food—we can and do. There is a time to fast and a time to feast. But periods of fasting enable us to break our compulsive preoccupation with food and to put food back in its place. In finding escape from the bondage to food, we often gain release from slavery to sensuality in other areas of life.

Jesus and fasting

Jesus fasted, taught us how to fast, and simply assumed we would do it. We do not have a record of how many times Jesus fasted, but it is fair to assume that his practices matched that of the Pharisees, the most outwardly pious people of that time. That would have included national fasts along with fasting on certain holy days and, as was common for Jews in those days, fasting two days each week. We have record of one long fast Jesus took. He fasted for forty days at the start of his ministry (see Matt. 4). If Jesus—God's Son, the incarnation of God—felt obligated to fast, who are we to consider this as an optional discipline?

There is one confusing Scripture related to fasting, however. Apparently, Jesus' disciples did not fast in the same way that the Pharisees and the disciples of John the Baptist did. In fact, some of John's disciples actually brought the matter to Jesus' attention (see Matt. 9:14–17). It is not clear whether Jesus' disciples never fasted or if they had simply skipped a particular traditional day of fasting. It is obvious, though, that they did not fast on some of the occasions when it was expected. Jesus defended their omission by pointing out that nobody fasts at a wedding feast. In other words, there is a time to fast and a time to celebrate. Jesus' reply is a reminder that fasting as a way of life is not our goal. We should never think that if we could only quit eating, we'd become really holy. If we quit eating altogether, we'd only become dead.

The church has a history packed with examples of radical fasting. Anthony, an early church leader known as one of the desert fathers, lived on only bread and water for decades. (Bread then was substantially more nutritious than what is available today.) But we are not trying to become desert hermits. Few people will read this chapter and then take fasting to excess. Our excess is to eat too much and fast too little. Fasting as a way of life is not the goal of this discipline. We need to know when to fast, and for what.

kinds of fasts

Fasting for the sake of fasting is only a little better than dieting. The reason we fast may contribute as much to the outcome as does the fasting itself. Perhaps the best use of fasting is for repentance for our own sins or the sins of others. This is the sort of fasting "in sackcloth and ashes" we see mentioned in the Bible. When a nation has sinned (or a church, denomination, or family), it turns to God in fasting to demonstrate its repentant heart. It is not that fasting earns forgiveness (nothing we can do accomplishes that), but fasting shows God that we are serious about sin and do not treat it casually. This sort of fast is something like penance and is rare today. When something goes wrong in our families or nations, we usually blame someone else, not ourselves and certainly not our own sins.

We might also fast to promote the discipline of *prayer*. Indeed, fasting and prayer are twin disciplines often practiced together. Fasting can cut away the spiritual fat around our hearts, enabling us to better focus on prayer. Fasting and prayer for another's salvation or healing is a common usage of this discipline.

Fasting as a means of *mourning* is so natural that when a loved one dies, those left behind almost always have to be urged to eat. Fasting during mourning also acts as a means of recovery from grief, perhaps even faster than other methods of grief recovery.

There are at least two more good purposes for fasting. One is fasting as a means of *identification* with Christ as we do during

Lent. We might also fast to identify with the millions of starving people in the world. Another purpose is to fast as a means of *escape* from sensuality. The connection between our inability to control our appetites for food and our appetites for sex has long been observed. The discipline we gain by fasting from food can have a spillover effect into other areas of life.

good hunger

This chapter is not suggesting that food and hunger are sinful. They are not. The self-denying life is not an automatic route to the holy life. Hunger is a good thing, and eating to satisfy hunger can glorify God. After all, whether we eat or drink, we are to do it all to the glory of God (1 Cor. 10:31). But when was the last time we were hungry—*really* hungry. What we call hunger usually isn't. Without knowing real hunger, we can never know real satisfaction. One of the gifts we receive from fasting is real hunger. The first bowl of broth after a long fast is far more satisfying than a choice steak. So in a curious way, fasting actually enhances our satisfaction with food; the process of fasting simplifies what it takes to satisfy us. But there is another hunger that emerges—a deep hunger for God. Remember Jesus' reply to Satan's temptation in the wilderness: "Man does not live on bread alone, but on every word that comes from the mouth of God" (Matt. 4:4). When fasting, our hunger for food reminds us to be hungry for the Word of God. Fasting can make us hungry for food but even hungrier for God.

peacefulness

Fasting can bring peacefulness to a harried life. Our lives are busy. We sprint from one appointment to the next, talking on our cell phones all the way, then rush off to meet someone else. We pick up the kids, drop them off at yet another place, go out for supper, pick up the kids again, then come home and collapse into an exhausted heap. And we wonder why we have no peace. While the discipline of rest has the most beneficial effect on our hectic lives, fasting also brings peace. The discipline of fasting is often melded with solitude, silence, Scripture, and prayer. It is *spiritual* fasting we are after. When we come down from our caffeine and sugar highs, we meet ourselves going the other way—more quiet and peaceful editions of the people who began the fast. God uses fasting to transform and recalibrate us.

dependence on God

Going without something makes us appreciate the very thing we've gone without; in the case of fasting—food. Food is a gift from God and should be seen that way. Jesus taught us to pray: "Give us today our daily bread" (Matt. 6:11). Daily bread is not a sin to avoid, but a gift for which to be grateful. This is why we say grace before meals—to return thanks to God. Even if we earned the salary that bought the food, we thank God for it because all good things come from him. Fasting is a way to remind ourselves that we are totally dependent upon God. We may think we have greater reserves of food than the sparrows outside the window, yet when there is a storm coming and the grocery store shelves are ransacked in a few hours, we realize how fragile our food supply is. Fasting reminds us that, like the sparrows, we would not have our daily bread if not for God's grace. After fasting we return to the table, saying grace with renewed meaning. God *is* great, and God *is* good, and we *do* thank him for our food. He is the source of all good things.

how to begin practicing fasting

start small

Fasting is like weight lifting. You wouldn't begin weight training by trying to lift a three-hundred-pound barbell. So when you try fasting, start small. As you develop spiritual muscle, add greater loads—that is, longer periods of fasting.

consider a partial fast

A total fast is abstaining from all food and drinking only water. Many longer fasts today are partial fasts, in which we abstain from only certain foods; or liquid fasts, in which we drink only simple fruit juices. Some people fast from chocolate, carbonated beverages, or beverages with caffeine. You might emulate many early Christians and Daniel, who refused to eat any meat, following a strict vegetarian diet (Dan. 1:12). Partial fasts like these can continue for years or even a lifetime. For centuries Christians abstained from red meat every Friday in order to remember the day Christ shed his blood. Partial fasts make the best impact when they are used as reminders, not merely to improve health or give evidence of self-denial. Perhaps you could assign some spiritual meaning to fasting from chocolate or caffeine. If you do, it will make for a better spiritual fast.

start a special-day fast

Early Christians fasted twice each week, on Wednesdays and Fridays. Such fasts usually ended at sundown and were frequent reminders of Christ's life and death—sort of like Ash Wednesdays and Good Fridays. If you were to pick a day to fast this week, which day would you pick? Why?

plan for the next Lent

Regardless of whether your denomination calls Lent by its name or uses some other name like Forty Days of Prayer and Fasting, consider what sort of a fast you might make this coming Lent. For two thousand years, Christians have fasted in some way during the time preceding Easter in order to meditate on Christ's suffering. On Easter weekend itself, most Christians fasted for forty hours between Good Friday and Easter Sunday morning. Then they celebrated Easter with a great feast, appropriately so, which ushered in a longer, fifty-day period of celebration—the season of Pentecost. What sort of fast might you make for this coming Lent? Is there a family tradition you might begin?

think about a major fast

In time you may aim to undertake a major fast for a week or longer. If so you will want to read more about fasting than what is contained in this chapter. Some people with medical conditions should not undertake a major fast. Check with your doctor first. In a major fast, you will experience reduced energy and the peacefulness you experience may be interpreted as illness or tiredness by your friends and coworkers. Read more on this discipline before you launch into a major fast. But for now, at least ask yourself if you might *ever* attempt such a fast.

what about you?

What are your specific plans to practice the discipline of fasting this week?

2. silence

*There is a time for everything, and a season for every activity
under heaven: . . . a time to be silent and a time to speak.*

—*Ecclesiastes 3:1, 7*

Silence is abstaining from sound in order to open our spiritual ears and listen more closely to the voice of God. God seldom speaks loudly. He usually speaks in a "still small voice," often little more than an impression in our minds (1 Kings 19:12 KJV). The clamor of modern life easily drowns out this soft voice of God. In the shelter of silence, it is easier to hear God's prompting.

silence as a hearing aid

The noisier our lives are, the harder it is to hear God. We can go for months—perhaps even years—without hearing God speak. It is possible to hear his words filtered through others (friends, preachers, or mentors) while going for a long time without directly hearing his prompting. Some have never heard it. While it is true that God does speak to us through others, he also prompts, urges, nudges, and communicates with us directly. Through the discipline of silence, we seek attentiveness to God's leading. Rarely does he speak in an audible voice, but God does guide us with an inner prompting and speaks to us personally through his Word. We can know for sure that he is leading us. We plan times of silence so we can better tune in to this quiet voice of God.

devaluation of words

The more words we hear and speak the less worth these words have. Modern life is crammed with words. We speak thousands of them each day and hear thousands more. Friends chatter about their weekends; bosses give instructions; family members talk about sports; neighbors chat about what's happening on their favorite TV shows. We Protestants have even taken sacred acts of worship like the Lord's Supper and filled them up with words. Our lives are packed with words! But words are like dollars; the more you make, the less each one is worth. Every word we speak or hear reduces the value of the rest. It is possible to fill our lives with so many words of our own that the words of God get lost in the white noise. Practicing the discipline of silence is a way to turn off the many words from our world so we can hear the fewer, more valuable words from God.

talking too much

The discipline of silence involves more than reducing the number of words we hear. It also includes cutting down on the number of words we say. How we love to talk! This is why good listeners are in such great demand. It is the law of supply and demand: there are far more good talkers than there are good listeners. This is especially true in the church. Most Christians run off at the mouth too much. The book of James suggests that improper use of speech may be the master sin—the hardest one to control. Proverbs, along with other Wisdom Literature, consistently condemns those who talk a lot and praises those who know how to remain silent. So when we seek silence, we not only fast from the voices of others, but also discipline ourselves to speak less. This is why (for some of us) the discipline of silence ought to be practiced by itself, not accompanied by prayer or journaling. When we pray or journal, we may merely be talking by another means. More of us should simply zip our lips and quietly listen for God's voice. Sometimes we ought to say nothing unless spoken to. We ought to be seen and not heard by God. For many in the church, the discipline of silence will be a difficult one, not because we will miss hearing others speak, but because we will miss hearing *ourselves* speak. But sometimes saying nothing is the best thing to say.

background noise

What passes for silence these days usually contains a lot of noise. A motorcycle passes the house; the neighbor's lawn mower has lost its muffler; a faraway truck downshifts noisily for a red light; a train whistles in the distance; an ambulance siren whines across town. These sounds are the background noises of modern life. And to them we willfully add noises of our own, sometimes claiming that our white noise will obliterate the clamor around us. As soon as we get into our cars, we switch on the radio. The moment we walk in the door, we turn on the TV. When we invite friends over, we insist on playing background music to banish silence from our homes. We fill up our lives with noise. The discipline of silence helps us escape the tyranny of noise and recalibrate our souls in stillness. In silence we seek to hear one voice—the voice of God. However, there is a catch: the voice of God is usually a silent one. If we want to hear him speak, we must be willing to wait. The foyer of silence prepares us to enter the presence of the King and hear from him.

silence and Scripture

The fact that we seek to hear God's voice does not mean that his promptings in our hearts are better than Scripture. Almost all of what God has to say, he has already said. Jesus said most of it, and the Bible says the rest. One reason we need silence is to allow God to enliven Scripture to us. God can speak to us by igniting a verse of the Bible or bringing to mind a scriptural phrase from a song. Indeed, silence is good preparation for reading the Scriptures. And silence is what we should allow following the reading so the Holy Spirit can apply that Scripture to our lives. Silence does not replace Scripture, but enhances and personalizes the guidance God gives through Scripture. Silence is also valuable when combined with prayer. How many times have we urgently prayed, then abruptly said amen and scurried away without waiting for God's answer? Practicing the discipline of silence provides time for listening to God after reading Scripture or praying. In silence we listen.

silence as an alloy

Silence is often used best in conjunction with other disciplines. (In fact, *all* of the disciplines are more effective when merged with other disciplines.) Silence helps us in reading Scripture, journaling, and praying. Silence is almost always a twin discipline with solitude—usually, when we are alone practicing solitude, we are also silent. There is, however, one way to practice silence without solitude, but it is difficult to do.

silence with others

It is possible to practice silence when we are with other people. Holding our tongues when we are with friends or coworkers is sometimes harder than keeping silent during solitude. We should only say what needs to be said when it needs to be said and nothing more. When we flee the noisy life and find refuge in silence, we discover that God himself is the quiet type. God often says nothing at all or very little. But when he does speak, his words are always the right thing said at the right time. We should become more like God when we are with others: saying less but with more meaning.

how to begin practicing silence

pick a time and place

When could you get away from your normal routine and sit in total silence? Where would you go? Schedule and do it, or go right now. Don't busy yourself by making preparations or taking Bible resources with you. Find a sanctuary of silence and quietly sit. In Europe many churches are left unlocked for this purpose.

You might find a place at your town library, tucked away among the shelves. If you are inclined to the outdoors, you may find a trail or pond hidden away from the noise and chatter of life. Where would you go? When could you do it? Will you?

displace distracting thoughts

When you first attempt to enter silence, your thoughts may try to shout you down. This is common for newcomers to this discipline. Learn to displace those noisy thoughts by concentrating on one thing, perhaps a Scripture passage or a story from the Bible.

find moments of silence in your day

Try something new this week by refusing to listen to the radio in your car. Or unplug your TV for a week and see how the atmosphere of your home changes. Maybe you will want to add garage moments to your life: each time you park your car in the garage, sit in silence for five minutes before going into the house. (Remember to turn off the engine or you may experience permanent silence!) Even if you do not have a chance to set aside a full day—or even an hour—for silence this week, you could create one of these moments of silence. Which one seems most attractive to you?

restrain your tongue in conversations

You could decide this week to speak half as much as you usually do and to listen more. In other words, each time you think of something to say, restrain yourself and keep listening (or only ask questions for clarification) so that you wind up saying only half of what you would normally say. Watch people's reactions and meditate on what their reactions tell you about yourself. Most of us should be able to go at least one week saying half what we normally say, right?

use your night watch

Do you wake at night and have a hard time falling back to sleep? If that happens this week, get up and go sit in a quiet place. Don't read anything; don't pray; don't do anything. Just purposely sit in the presence of the Lord. When you get sleepy again, go back to bed. See what a difference this makes the next morning.

try a half-day's silence

Perhaps you are fortunate enough to be able to spend four full hours in silence this week, just sitting before the Lord. If so, you may experience the greatest impact in your life. Don't try to make this time "worthwhile" by doing too much. The only people we can sit in silence with are those we love, so sit silently with God. He loves you and you love him. Just *be* together.

what about you?

What are your specific plans to practice the discipline of silence this week?

3. solitude

*At daybreak Jesus went out to a solitary place. The people were
looking for him and when they came to where he was,
they tried to keep him from leaving them.*

—Luke 4:42

Solitude is abstaining from contact with people in order to be
alone with God and grow closer to him. It is fasting from social
contact in order to remove others from the God-and-me equation.
The value of solitude is that it closes off many relationships
so we can focus on one. It has been said that church father
Diadochos of Photiki observed that if the door of a steam bath
is continuously left open, the inside heat escapes. Likewise,
he suggested, spending too much time with the doors of our
lives open to other people permits the heat of our souls to
escape. There is a time to close the door to other relationships in
order to open ourselves to the most important relationship—the
one with God.

fasting from friendships

Friendship is a good thing. So is community. Yet when we practice the discipline of solitude, we forgo the companionship of friends in order to experience a better companionship with God. Solitude is taking away time from others to spend time alone with God. We might survive without friendships. We cannot survive without God. Solitude does not reduce the value of friendship but teaches us to more deeply appreciate those relationships. Doing without any useful thing only reminds us of how much we need it. Absence makes the heart grow fonder, as the saying goes. Solitude reminds us of the order we should maintain in our relationships— God first, others second. A Christian who does not practice solitude is likely to be over-reliant on friends and under-reliant on God. Solitude corrects this imbalance.

fear of being alone

Why do many of us fear being alone? Is it loneliness we dread? Maybe not, because it is possible to be lonely in the company of others or to experience no loneliness when alone. Being lonely is not the same as being alone. In the discipline of solitude, we arrange to be alone with God so that we do not have to be lonely with others. Maybe we fear being alone because we fear being exposed. Solitude (and its companion discipline, silence) has a way of stripping us. Most of us fear being alone with ourselves—we don't like the company. And some of us fear being alone with God—he knows too much about us. We cannot hide from him. If we do not feel fully forgiven and accepted by God, being alone with him can be terrifying, like a trip to the principal's office. Maybe that's why some of us fill our lives with noisy friendships: to avoid being left alone with *the* Principal. But we have nothing to fear in coming alone into God's presence. He is a loving God who knows us better than we know ourselves. Indeed, in times of solitude, we can come to know ourselves as God knows us. And over time, we can come to accept ourselves as God accepts us.

community life

The person who cannot stand to be alone is a danger to a group. What do you bring to any group other than yourself? People who cannot be alone should be suspect to the church. There is something wrong inside them. Is this why there is something wrong in the church today? Are we a people craving community who cannot be alone? It is hopeless to find refuge in community while fleeing solitude. It is when we are alone with God that we find him—and ourselves—and can thus return to our communities renewed and realigned to contribute what we have gained in solitude.

Jesus and the early Christians

Jesus and the early Christians practiced solitude. Just before he began his ministry, Jesus spent a full forty days and nights in the solitude of the desert. He emerged in power. Even though he had only a few years to accomplish his earthly work, Jesus arranged his life so that he could slip away from his followers sometimes to be alone. Many of the earliest Christians took solitude so seriously they went into the desert to devote themselves full time to prayer and study. These desert fathers or desert hermits made great contributions to our understanding of Christianity today. They considered time alone with God so critical that they gave their whole lives to it. Most Christians today dismiss these desert fathers as extremists. But our excess today is in the opposite direction—spending too much time with others and not enough time with God. When we escape the social busyness of our modern world to spend time alone with God, we enter into the recesses of God's own solitude. After all, God himself both embodies community in the Trinity and is solitary in his separateness from us.

solitude and self-definition

In solitude, God corrects our self-definition. All of society conspires to define us in terms of *doing*, *having*, and *relationships*. In our social interchange, we ask, "What do you do?" Or we notice people's possessions and make an estimate of them accordingly. Or we ask questions to discover who they are related to, then assign labels to them such as "Tim's wife" or "Amber's assistant" or "our state senator." Society would have us believe that we are nothing more than the sum of what we do, what we have, and who we are connected to. In solitude, God corrects this aberration and assigns a new definition to us based on our *being*. Having a properly aligned sense of self enables us to return to society with purpose and peace and reconnect with our work, our things, and our relationships in a better way.

how to begin practicing solitude

find a place

If you want to try this discipline, the first step is to conceive of a place where you might go—a hermitage. Do you remember a hideout you had as a child? Now find one as an adult. If you were going to fast from contact with people for several hours, where would you go to find solitude?

schedule a time

Set a nonnegotiable appointment with God and stick with it. Don't cancel on God.

keep your expectations sensible

Don't expect wild visions and sparkling insight in a few hours. Expect to wind down a bit and sense you are in God's "waiting room."

keep the focus on God

It is possible to be alone in solitude without sensing that you are in God's presence. Time alone has some benefits, but time alone with God is better. Work at turning your alone time into God time.

seek one important message from God

If you have not regularly been practicing this discipline as a means of grace, don't expect God to unload everything he has wanted to say to you for years in your first hour together. He is more likely to unfold his words to you over time. At the most, expect only one clear impression each time you meet with him.

be aware of effect lag

You may not notice the effect of solitude immediately. The effect may not come for days or even weeks. Give this discipline time to change you. Actually, it isn't the discipline at all; you are giving God himself time to work.

seek moments of solitude in your day

If you decide to skip this discipline (and you shouldn't), at least try seeking moments of solitude within your regular, daily schedule. You might follow up this reading by treating your daily commute differently. Or plan a walk by yourself this week. Or after supper one night, go sit on the porch for an hour or two, or close the door to your bedroom for a half hour in the morning and lie awake, alone with God. For just one week, you might decide that every time you park your car you'll take a full five minutes of solitude before getting out.

try longer time periods

All of the disciplines are not for all the people all of the time. If you discover that the discipline of solitude is a powerful means of spiritual formation in your life, try it for a longer period: perhaps a full day or even a whole week. You don't need to become a full-time hermit to experience the spiritually trans-forming power of this discipline, but at least try it *some* time.

what about you?

What are your specific plans to practice the discipline of solitude this week?

4. simplicity

*Do not store up for yourselves treasures on earth, where moth
and rust destroy, and where thieves break in and steal.*

—*Matthew 6:19*

Simplicity is intentionally paring down our lifestyles to the essentials in order to free ourselves from the tyranny of things and to focus more on spiritual life. Few disciplines go more against the grain of our culture yet provide greater freedom than this one. The simple life is easier and less-complicated to live, and it enables us to direct attention to the most important things. By practicing simplicity, we abandon our preoccupation with the latest gadgets, styles, and must-have symbols of success and embrace more lasting things. In a culture that preaches piling up treasure as the route to happiness, simplicity is our statement of objection. It says that we believe happiness is not found in the abundance of our possessions but in the fewness of our wants. When we practice this discipline, we find the freedom and joy of an uncomplicated life. We come to have a single vision, and our focus is increasingly on God and eternal things rather than ourselves and material things.

our simplicity heritage

Jesus is the ultimate example of simplicity. What were his possessions? Where was his home? What forms of transportation did he use? Gandhi is often honored for his simple life that enabled him to carry everything he owned in a linen bag. Jesus did not even have a bag. His legacy was a simple, seamless garment—and a worldwide religion. Jesus' disciples took on the discipline of simplicity too. The early church grew as Christ's followers sold their possessions and served others. Congregations sprung up that became known for sharing possessions and caring for widows and orphans. People were attracted to these communities of love in which people acted as if material possessions were not very important. The Christians in Jerusalem did not treat their possessions as their own, and that example typified the early church for several hundred years. The desert fathers denied themselves all the comforts of life in order to focus on their relationships with God. Later in history, for more than a thousand years, monasteries became places where individuals abandoned the worries brought by having personal possessions and gave themselves to worship, study, and service. Simplicity has a long history in the church and is traced right back to Jesus Christ himself. When we take up this discipline, we join a long line of dedicated Christians.

temporal idolatry

We might ask, "Shouldn't the Christian life be one of celebration and happiness, not a stern life of denial?" Of course the Christian life is one of joy. Our error is in believing that material possessions bring this sort of joy. We are told by our culture that we can achieve happiness by collecting the possessions that typify the "good life." But possessions all turn to dust and rust. In time we discover that we are no happier than when we had nothing. Maybe we are even less happy. We sit surrounded by our piles of possessions but have empty souls. Happiness and freedom are not found in an abundance of possessions but in a simple life of trust. The more we possess, the more we will rely on our possessions and the less we will rely on God. Materialism sets itself up as an idol in the temple of our hearts proclaiming, "The spiritual world has no value—you can't eat it, wear it, or live in it." To tear down this idol, we adopt habits of simplicity that affirm eternal and spiritual values, dethroning the material. Like a tiny drop of poison added to our coffee each day, materialism slowly poisons the soul.

Surrounded by possessions, dimness of soul eventually becomes normal. After a while, we no longer even know what it is like to sense the deeper and more important things of life. However, when we intentionally reject the falsehoods of the material life and practice simplicity—even a little bit—we are freed from the tyranny of the temporal world. In the process, we become reacquainted with spiritual and eternal things.

mutiny of possessions

We pile up possessions so they can serve us, yet we eventually become servants to the things we own. Our culture teaches us that the material world matters most, so we collect possessions that are supposed to satisfy the soul. But we experience a strange disappointment once we have these things. They do not measure up to their advertisements. As a result, we constantly believe that the *next* thing will satisfy us more. This is the treadmill of materialism. The more things we collect, the less satisfied we become. It is like drinking seawater: the more we drink, the thirstier we get. Finally, we realize that a strange thing has happened—our possessions have come to possess us. The garage door opener breaks and commands us to arrange for its repair. The lawn mower does not start and orders us to get it fixed. The car insists that we schedule a trip to change its oil. And we obey. There has been a mutiny! Our possessions have taken over! We are no longer the captains of our ships but have been made galley slaves by our own belongings—we now work for them. We are possessions of our possessions, slaves of our slaves. By taking on habits of simplicity, we break free of the tyranny of the material and regain control from the things that have come to run our lives.

breaking free

The older we are the harder it is to escape bondage to material possessions. Collecting becomes a habit. After decades it is a hard habit to beak. We pile up things until we move to a nursing home or die. Then our children toss out our junk, shaking their heads and asking, "Now why did they keep *that*?" Adopting habits of simplicity helps us to rotate stock—it gets rid of our old stuff as new stuff comes in. Better yet, simplicity discards possessions without replacing them. When we adopt habits of simplicity, we break loose from the burden of having too many things and experience the joy of traveling light. Sometimes we simply have to walk away from some very large things to find joy.

frugality, poverty, and simplicity

Of course, all of us can't take a vow of poverty—and we shouldn't. The evil is not in things themselves but in our excessive absorption with them. Taking up habits of simplicity breaks that bondage. The classic approach to this discipline offers three related exercises. First, there is *frugality*, the careful use of money in providing necessities in order to get the greatest value. The frugal person gets the best bang for the buck, or better yet, doesn't spend the buck at all if the thing isn't really needed. However, as good as frugality is, it is not by itself a virtue. Materialists can be frugal while only saving up more for themselves. Indeed, most misers are frugal. Frugality is good only if placed in the service of generosity.

A second exercise is *voluntary poverty*. In this case, the emphasis is not on being poor so much as on *choosing* poverty. Some monks make that choice in the form of three vows: poverty, chastity, and obedience (thus addressing three great temptations of life—money, sex, and power). They abstain from personal ownership of anything at all. Few of us could be so radical unless we lived in some sort of commune. And even if we did, we still might not become totally free of materialism. Many monks eventually faced a dimness of soul because they merely replaced personal materialism with collective materialism—some religious orders became extremely wealthy over time. Although the members made vows of poverty, the order owned all kinds of lavish possessions for their use. So even with a vow of poverty, materialism can be a snare.

We should probably all practice some frugality. And a few of us may even take a vow of poverty. But every one of us can practice the third exercise, *simplicity*—intentionally reducing the hold that material things have on us by owning fewer things. As we do, we clear away the clutter from our lives, find God, and learn to trust him better.

relative simplicity

Where can we find the sensible middle ground on simplicity? We can't all become monks. We have families to provide for, retirement to consider, and other obligations to address. But how much is too much? How far should we go in dismantling our treasure on earth? Certainly this discipline must be tailored to each person individually. What would be considered moderate simplicity to a Christian in Burma might look like abject poverty to a Christian in suburban Chicago. Living a simple life in North Carolina might seem to be a wantonly excessive lifestyle to a Christian in Bangladesh. Even among friends attending the same local church there will be varying tolerations for simplicity. "Oh, I could never do without that" is what we say when describing what we think of as a necessity. But one person's necessity may be another's luxury. So we will each have to apply this discipline personally and be careful of being judgmental about how others live. Most of us feel the grip of materialism and sense our own addiction to nice things. Taking even small steps to reverse the clutch of materialism can bring some freedom. And freedom breeds more freedom. Once we start on this path, turning back is unlikely. Certainly no one can set absolute standards for others, but that doesn't mean we do not need to set standards for ourselves. Simplicity may be relative, but it is not optional—at least for the people following Jesus Christ, who taught such radical notions about possessions.

simplicity as moderation

As with so many solutions, moderation is the key to applying the discipline of simplicity. When we adopt this discipline, we will not, for example, toss out all our clothes and keep only a single change of attire. That may have worked in Jesus' time, but few of us seriously think even Jesus would dress that way in today's world. For most of us, simplicity of dress has to do more with *moderation* than *essentials*. If we were concerned only with what is essential for life, then of course one set of clothing would be adequate. But few of us could survive in modern life on only the bare essentials. Our world doesn't work that way. The discipline of simplicity moves us *toward* the essentials. It is a journey against materialism that most of us will never complete. At least we won't complete the journey until death, the final downsizing. All downsizing we do before then is only preparation. We will take nothing with us. Yes, we need some things now—probably more things than Jesus had. But how many changes of clothing do we need? How many pairs of shoes do we own? Five? Ten? Twenty? More? Do we need so many? Practicing the discipline of simplicity leads us to determine how much we really need and moves us toward having only what we need and nothing more. Taking on this discipline in our modern world is more about moderation than total abstinence. In simplicity, we abstain from material excess, from collecting things as if they provided happiness and meaning. Only God can give us the happiness and meaning we crave.

following the heart

We should remind ourselves that possessions themselves are not wrong; it is loving our possessions that brings danger. The problem is that we can't serve two masters—God and possessions. Jesus said it clearly. He taught us that our hearts follow our treasures. It is hard for the heart to care about eternal, spiritual things when it is caring about temporal, material ones. This is why we practice simplicity—to break free from the mastery of materialism and refocus our eyes on God. And in ridding ourselves of the things we thought would make us happy, we find truer and deeper happiness in him.

how to begin practicing simplicity

don't start collecting things

Are you a single person or young couple who owns little more than a stack of CDs, a worn-out computer, and two old chairs you got from your aunt? Do you have far more debt than you're worth, and would all your possessions still fit in the back seat of your beat-up car? Then applying this discipline will be easy for you. Simply *stay* simple. Decide now what sort of lifestyle is sensible and determine to not surpass it. Write down a description of your ideal lifestyle and put it in your Bible so you can remember it years from now when you are able to afford a moving van load of things.

say no to spending

Pick one purchase every day and say no to it, even something as small as a soft drink. Do this not because buying things is wrong, but to break your bondage to the notion that a purchase will make you happier.

give away things

Walk through your house with boxes and take out things you have not used in a year, or two years, or whatever time limit you think is reasonable. If you have not worn a sweater in a year, should you really keep it? If that tool has not been used for two years, why hoard it? Gather a pile of unused possessions somewhere, but not in the attic. Give away these things. Voluntary poverty (a form of simplicity) is not just doing without things; it is a means of being generous.

have a garage sale

Perhaps a garage sale is the way to toss out your extra baggage. Having one of your own, that is, not visiting one at your neighbor's house to collect more stuff! Some Christians have a garage sale every year and give the income to support world evangelism or another charity.

get rid of leftovers from your last move

Do you still have unpacked boxes from your last move or even from two moves ago? If so, schedule an hour this week (and every week until you are finished) to sort, discard, or give away those things. Your children will only have to do it anyway when you go into a nursing home. If now is not a good time to start, when will be better? Do you really think you'll be better able to do it when you're middle-aged, retired, or just before you enter a nursing home?

plan a backpacking trek

Most of us are unable to continually practice severe simplicity as John the Baptist, Jesus, and the early church fathers did. But we can experience it for a short time by taking a backpacking trek. If you are physically able, consider going for a week or more carrying only necessities on your back. Then watch how what you thought were necessities turn into luxuries once you have to carry them around all day! Let this become a lesson for life. Few experiences today are as similar to first-century simplicity as backpacking.

begin downsizing

If you agree that an overabundance of possessions is actually a burden, then you might take simplicity even more seriously and begin to downsize your lifestyle in a serious way. Give away the extra furniture cluttering your house to a young couple or to the Salvation Army. Find a young person who has no tools and give away your extra set of socket wrenches or your only set if you have not been using it. Get rid of all that stuff in your storage locker. Why pay rent to store things that will eventually be tossed? Check the attic, garage, and basement of your house asking, "Why should I keep this?" Give yourself permission to buy things again if you find out later that you need them later. Consider moving into a smaller house that will make you automatically downsize. Again, do not take up this discipline because having little will make you holy. Do it because having fewer things will free you to be happier, and do it in order to give to those in need. This act will be a testimony that the spiritual things are more important to you than material ones. And it will bring you closer to God.

what about you?

What are your specific plans to practice the discipline of simplicity this week?

5. rest

By the seventh day God had finished the work he had been doing;
so on the seventh day he rested from all his work. And God blessed
the seventh day and made it holy, because on it he rested
from all the work of creating that he had done.

—Genesis 2:2–3

In the discipline of rest, we retreat from the frantic pace of life in order to be physically and spiritually restored. The practice of this discipline involves taking off days from work, going on vacations, and getting a full night's sleep *every* night. Rest is the antidote for workaholism. This discipline is an emerging one that was less critical in the slower-paced Middle Ages, but is essential in modern times. Christians who ignore rest are often proud that they do, but they pay a price. In rest, God restores the body, mind, and soul—all three of which are interrelated. After the proper practice of rest, we are able to return to a high velocity life with renewed strength, clearer purpose, and recalibrated priorities. Rest is a tune-up for us. It lets us unwind so that we run more efficiently when we return to activity.

the discipline of laziness

Most successful people fail at one important discipline — the discipline of laziness. *Laziness* is always a bad word as far as most of us are concerned. Indeed, if sloth is our major personal temptation, then we should skip this chapter completely. But if we are like most modern Christians, we sometimes experience the barrenness of the busy life. We rush about frantically even as we complain about our hyperactive pace. The fact that we are taking life at a furious speed proves to us that we are having fun and doing worthwhile things. In activity, we find meaning. At supper we ask one another, "So, what did you do today?" We open our Sunday school classes by asking, "Let's go around and tell what we each did this weekend?" If we answer, "Nothin' much; I just sat around and vegged," we'll see horrified expressions or hear bursts of laughter. Doing nothing is bad, according to some modern Christians, but doing something — anything — is considered good. So we cram our lives full of busyness to convince our friends and ourselves that we are having a good time. By taking up the spiritual discipline of rest, we force ourselves to lie down in green pastures, to practice what some have called the "discipline of laziness," for a time. Rest includes both a good day off and a good night's sleep.

hooked on hurry

Some of us have a more serious malady: We are addicted to hurry. We rush from one double-booked appointment to the next, making quick calls to cover our late arrivals. We dash around panting so that everyone knows they should not interrupt us because we're too busy. Someone asks, "How's it going?" and we respond, "Oh, I'm just *so* busy." But we love it. The exciting pace of our lives gives us the same rush people get by speeding over railroad crossings to beat oncoming trains. It may be dangerous, but it's exhilarating if you live to tell about it. This malady has no cure but one—the discipline of rest. The only exit from the 24/7 rat race is enforced laziness, the setting aside of Sabbath time.

cease and desist

The idea of ceasing work came long before the Ten Commandments; it is rooted in creation. Genesis 2:2 reports that following creation, God himself took a day off. What a curious claim! Was God so worn out that he needed to catch up on sleep? Why would God cease work on the seventh day? You'd think that if God were truly God, he could work twenty-four hours a day without getting worn out, wouldn't you? Yet Genesis shows God taking a day off. Perhaps we are told this to remind us that taking time off is built into creation itself. It is not an option.

God didn't have to design the world this way. He could have created us so that we need no sleep at all. Without the need to rest, we could work for his kingdom constantly—all day, all night, all year long. How much more we'd get done! Wouldn't God have gotten more bang for his buck by creating no-rest humans? We don't know why, but he didn't. He made us as creatures that need rest. Much of the natural world is similar—there is both summer and winter, seasons of growth and dormancy, years for planting and letting the ground lie fallow. For humans God designated the boundary between work and rest, sleep and wakefulness, and he expects us to wisely budget between them. If we had written Genesis 2:2, we'd have God rushing off after a week's work to water ski all day at the lake then catch a movie before going out for dinner—that's what we call a day off. In the real Genesis, God simply rests, ceases work, and *does nothing*.

Rest is more than a once-a-week discipline. Jesus once curled up for a nap in a boat during a powerful storm. Our need for rest is designed into the created order, and tampering with it is hazardous to our bodies, minds, and souls.

the Sabbath Sunday

Given the fact that God has designed us with the need for a day off every week, which day should it be? For many of us, the true seventh day of the week, Saturday, might be a good day on which to rest. Yet there are so many household duties piled up by Saturday that it may be difficult to rest at home. And if we go away for the day, we sometimes get caught up in rushed recreation and come home more exhausted than before we left. Yet Saturday, for many people, is the day to cease labor.

Sunday is perhaps more ideal for some because the rhythm of our culture calls for reduced work on that day. However, some church's Sunday schedules are so demanding that even this becomes another pressure-filled, rushed day—that is almost always true for pastors. The particular day we choose as our cease-and-desist day is not so important as the fact that we choose a day, *any* day. The Sabbath principle is a law written into creation. Making time to obey this law is not legalism; it is survival.

rest as a means of grace

Rest is God's ordained means of physically and spiritually restoring us. We should not challenge his design. We shouldn't, but we sometimes do. We work continuously, sometimes for months on end, without taking a real day off. We learn to get by on less than a full night's sleep, rise exhausted, and gulp down enough coffee to enable us to function all day. We use prescription drugs to defy the law of rest and survive for months or even years. Some college students live a sleep-deprived life, considering it "normal" for four years straight. To be honest, we must admit that we can defy the laws God established in nature. But the payment will eventually come due.

Going without proper sleep and regular days off changes us. At first we lose short-term memory and don't remember where we put things. Then we start forgetting appointments and feeling drowsy in meetings. We become crabby, irritable, and impatient with others. People start to avoid us and say, "Boy, they sure are touchy." Our minds slowly deteriorate, relationships degenerate, and spiritual passion dims. Fatigue leaves us open to all kinds of temptation, and we are not able to resist. When prisoners of war are interrogated, their captors use a standard technique to melt down the captives' will to resist. They deprive the prisoners of sleep. Fatigue weakens the will. We might seek counseling or pray for deliverance from irritability or weak will. But we do not need to go to the altar; we need to go to bed. God has ordained sleep. It can be a means of grace to restore, refresh, cleanse, and strengthen us. We dare not think we can abuse our bodies without affecting our hearts; they are interconnected. God can work in us while we are sleeping and while we are resting on a day off. Refusing to receive this means of grace cuts us off from God's work.

while you can

It could be that we resist the discipline of rest because we do not believe strongly enough in heaven. Have we come to believe the old slogan: "You only go around once, so grab all the gusto you can"? Do we really believe that this life is all there is—there is nothing more? Have we become practical materialists? Do we fear that the only time we have may be *this* time, these hours, this weekend, so we'd better cram our schedules full before our time runs out? Perhaps we imagine heaven (if we imagine it at all) as the ultimate day of rest and are determined to do our work now (and have our fun now) because there will be neither work nor fun in heaven. If we do, that thinking illustrates how pagan we have become. But what if heaven is a place of work—without weariness? Or what if heaven is a place of fun with such wonderful joy that it wouldn't even compare to water skiing or backpacking? What if heaven is like a life of stimulating conversations, wonderful dining, and all the things we now rush through on weekends? In other words, what if this life *isn't* all we get? Would that cause us to take a less frantic approach to the coming week? Maybe we all should stop reading this chapter right now and go take a much-needed nap!

how to begin practicing rest

quit apologizing

Decide to go all week without apologizing for resting. If someone calls on Sunday afternoon and asks, "Were you sleeping?" just tell them yes. If you take a lazy day this week, try to find some way to tell others, and do so without any twinge of guilt. When your Sunday school class asks, "What exciting thing did you do this weekend?" answer, "I rested," and refuse to be intimidated by any disappointment. Someone has to break the conspiracy to dismiss God's plan for rest; it may as well be you.

schedule a nap

Pick a time this week (or a time every day this week) for a short nap to let God refresh your soul and body. Set an alarm so you won't sleep too long and get groggy.

turn over a new leaf

Feeling drowsy in meetings or during a sermon is a classic sign of sleep deprivation. Most adults require between seven and nine hours of sleep each night. You can survive on less sleep if you are willing to pay the price (and if those around you are willing to pay it too). If you are not getting enough sleep, decide this week—even if only for this week—to get a full night's sleep every night. If you are a night owl, you may have to set an alarm clock to *go* to bed, and have the discipline to obey it. Watch how you change, even in one week.

examine your hobbies

Busy recreational activities are not wrong, but they are not rest either. Take this week to reflect on your hobbies and recreational activities. Is there balance between your rest and your recreation? If all your recreation is active, perhaps you should consider balancing it with a more restful activity. If you groan and say, "I can't imagine myself just sitting there doing nothing," you may be addicted to hurry and in all the more need of slow-paced recreation.

take a day off to do nothing

Determine to take a full day off this week to do nothing—a day of rest. Set only one goal: to do nothing. Measure your success in resisting work. Submit to God's command to cease work and take a real Sabbath. Reflect (but not too intensely) on how you are feeling. Don't read, journal, or *do* anything at all. Just lie down in green pastures and rest. See if God does anything in you while you are sitting, lying, and napping.

what about you?

What are your specific plans to practice the discipline of rest this week?

humility
servitude
loving

6. secrecy

Jesus' brothers said to him, "You ought to leave here and go to Judea, so that your disciples may see the miracles you do. No one who wants to become a public figure acts in secret. Since you are doing these things, show yourself to the world."

—*John 7:3–4*

The discipline of secrecy is abstaining from taking credit for the good deeds we do. When we practice secrecy, we arrange to do good things in such a way that others can't even find out who did them. Secrecy avoids receiving credit for doing good. It keeps others from concluding that our good works are evidence that we are good or spiritual people. When we take up the discipline of secrecy, we rely on God alone for our affirmation and approval. That strengthens our Father-child relationship with him and weakens our thirst for human approval.

a culture of credit

We live in a culture of credit. We are preoccupied with giving credit when credit is due and, more often, *taking* credit when credit is due. Most of our nonprofit organizations have learned that they must give recognition to their significant donors to maintain their funds. Large gifts are recognized with an announcement, press release, or gold plate, permanently advertising the giver's generosity. Everybody gets to know how generous we are. If they could pull it off without appearing too crude, some Christian organizations would probably arrange to have trumpets sound when announcing great gifts, just as some Pharisees did in Bible times! It is just how we do things. Because we live in a culture of credit, some of our churches have stained-glass windows with people's names on them. We have sidewalks with bricks that display givers' names for generations to come. We screw gold plates engraved with donors' names to just about everything in our churches and educational institutions. Almost every Christian college in the country annually publishes the names of their donors, organized by the amount given, so everyone will know who is most generous. Of course, when we do this, we totally ignore the teachings of Jesus. Why does the church so easily dismiss Jesus' clear intent in this matter? Because, as every fund-raiser knows, "People won't give if they don't get credit."

the thirst for recognition

Perhaps the reason we want credit so much is that we aren't completely confident we'll get credit later. We want recognition now because we are earthbound in our thinking. Sure, we know that Jesus promised recognition in heaven, but that is far off and ethereal. Who knows for sure if it will really happen? When churches praise us here and now, we can bask in the honor.

Public giving is like a scratch-off ticket—it pays off immediately. Getting credit here is our hedge fund of recognition—in case our later reward doesn't pan out. Being earthly minded creatures, we opt to take our credit now instead of hoping to get it later. This is why the discipline of secrecy is so powerful (though admittedly rare) in the church. Practicing secrecy forces us to shift focus from earth to heaven and from others to God. Secrecy makes us bet the farm on the existence of an afterlife in which God will reward people. If there is no heaven and no God, then we've lost our only chance for reward. This is why secrecy is vital as a means of spiritual formation—it is a potent statement of faith.

vainglory

The desert fathers called vainglorious those things we say or do to gain the admiration of others. Vainglory is a kind of vanity, a seeking to glorify the self. Praise from others bolsters our self-esteem. The discipline of secrecy is the cure for vainglory. Secrecy forces us to seek affirmation only from the One who knows us best and loves us most: our Father in heaven.

now or then

Jesus said we have a choice of either getting a reward now on earth or receiving it later in heaven. About those who sought credit on earth, he said, "They have received their reward in full" (Matt. 6:2). He taught us that we can actually store up treasure in heaven by quietly doing good deeds and not taking credit for them. If we do our good deeds to get credit here on earth, we will receive no reward for them in heaven. It is our choice: either get credit here now or there later. So are the fund-raisers right? Is it true that people won't give without getting credit? Is it true of *us*? Or are we better people than our fund-raisers think?

motivation

By warning us against taking credit for our good works, Jesus was not telling us we could never do a good deed that others might see, nor was he saying that we lose all credit from God if we get credit here. He was talking more about our motivation—*why* we do good. If we do good things merely in order to get noticed by others, then we lose our heavenly reward. It is our motivation that makes the deed either praiseworthy or hypocritical. So are our motives pure? Most of us will have to admit that we have mixed motivations. That is, even if we donate money out of pure altruism, when the givers' list is published, we search for our names (and the names of our peers). Taking credit may not be the original motivation, but it can sneak in later. Or our motives might be 90 percent pure, 50 percent, or they might vary depending on the situation. Secrecy provides a way to purify our motives, which is what it's all about. When practicing the discipline of secrecy, we carefully arrange *not* to get credit. Secrecy is anonymous giving and anonymous doing. In such secret actions, there can be no reward except from our Father in heaven. Secrecy tests our motivation. We get no receipt, no thank-you letter, no hug from the recipient, and no name printed on a list. Nobody has cause to believe that we are good or generous people when they hear of what we've done because they never hear of it. Our friends and spouses do not know. Nobody knows except for God. Is that enough?

secret piety

But secrecy is not just about giving alms to help people; it applies to acts of piety as well. Consider Jesus' teaching on fasting. He taught that when we fast we should make ourselves appear as if we haven't fasted at all. It is almost as if he was teaching us a sort of holy deception. This teaching shows how seriously Jesus condemned spiritual show-offs. What is true of fasting is true of all spiritual disciplines. While reading this book and when practicing some of these disciplines, we could be tempted to make a display of it. We might be tempted to say, "No thanks, I'm fasting this week," or, "I took a day of solitude and silence yesterday, and it was *so* empowering to my spiritual life." When we say such things, we might not even notice how we've staked out the spiritual high ground in the conversation. But others notice.

The discipline of secrecy extends beyond the giving of money to include the practice of secret piety. Ironically, we could practice all the disciplines in this book with great success but be worse off in God's eyes—if we did it only to make a spiritual display or if we became proud of our spiritual attainment. Sure, in a group where others are practicing the disciplines, it is helpful and appropriate to share our stories. Most groups that study this book will do that every week. But putting our habits of piety on display for people outside our study group can waste any gain we've made by their practice. God and a small group of friends will know of our secret piety. That should be enough.

secret needs

In addition to secret giving and secret piety, there is a third way some great saints have practiced this discipline—by keeping their *needs* secret. George Müeller is perhaps the best-known example of this kind of secrecy. Müeller founded a string of orphanages across England in the 1800s and started 117 schools where 120,000 young people were educated. Yet Müeller never made known any needs for these institutions, except to God. Müeller directed all his fund-raising appeals to one address: the throne of God. More than seven million dollars was supplied over his lifetime. Sometimes the children in the orphanages actually said grace over their empty plates and then, someone would bring in food, saying, "We just thought to bring this. What a coincidence!"

It is no secret that as much as half of the funds raised by some Christian organizations are spent on the fund-raising effort itself, and the percentage is even greater for many TV appeals. But if all Christian organizations today took Müeller's approach, how would we respond? Would we be sensitive enough to the Spirit's promptings to give? For ministries like Müeller's to work, it requires both a leader who doesn't ask for money *and* a people so sensitive to the Spirit that they'll obey his promptings without being asked. Maybe practicing secrecy in the area of need is only for the Green Berets of God's army—those elite troops who really do take God's Word at face value and believe that he will "meet all [our] needs according to his glorious riches" (Phil. 4:19). Few of us place *that* much trust in God. Perhaps more of us should.

exposing and correcting our values

Practicing secrecy exposes the extent to which we rely on receiving positive feedback from others, and it enables us to correct that situation. Without secrecy, we conclude that we are good because others say so. We believe we are generous because we can see our names on receipts or lists of donors. We figure that we must be good people because everyone says so when praising the good deeds we've done. We believe these things because we keep hearing them, and they may, in fact, be true. The problem is not the truth of these notions so much as their *source*. There is no good thing we can do that will make God love us more. There is no gift we can give to gain his love. He loves us not for what we do or give. Yet he does rejoice when we give generously and do good deeds. He is proud of us like a parent who posts a child's coloring page on the refrigerator door. But when we seek approval from others more than from our Father, our work is posted on the wrong refrigerator. The discipline of secrecy enables us to sanctify our good acts and gifts, setting them apart for God alone to approve. After all, God's approval is more important to us than the praise of people, isn't it?

how to begin practicing secrecy

make a list

Start by listing a few ideas for the practice of secrecy this week. Perhaps the easiest way to practice secrecy is to anonymously give cash to someone in need. But think of other ideas as well. Consider how you might do good for someone without anyone else finding out.

create a reminder

Design some way to remind yourself to practice this discipline in the course of normal life. Put it someplace where you will see it daily and be reminded to take secret action.

watch out for vainglory

Keep watch for indicators of your hunger to take credit. Notice the number of times you think, "Hey, nobody noticed what I did," or, "Why do *they* get so much attention for what they do?" or, "Doesn't anybody care what I do around here?" Use each incident as an occasion to pray, "I know *you* are watching, God, and that is enough for me today."

abstain from idea credit

Maybe you want to receive credit for your ideas like your giving or good deeds. This week purposely avoid taking credit for your ideas. Shun saying, "That was my idea, you know." Figure out how to plant ideas in others, and when they blossom, refuse to take any credit for them, even for planting the seed.

gracefully take recognition

If you receive recognition this week for something, take it gracefully with a short thank-you. Avoid playing self-centered games that are merely contrived to gain greater recognition. Refrain from saying, "Oh, it was nothing at all." Just say, "Thanks." Don't say, "I want to thank all the other people who helped me achieve this." Simply say, "Thank you." Avoid saying, "I was thinking as I heard these speeches that I really don't deserve this honor." Just say . . . well, you know what to say by now.

don't report next week

Normally, a group or class studying this book reports on experiences from the previous week. Skip that report next week. If your group or class wants to know what God has been doing within the group, simply have each person write on cards what they did, without their names, and then read the comments aloud. But even that may detract from the effect of this discipline because one could all take credit for what was done by the group. Perhaps the best plan is to simply let God be the audience this week.

what about you?

What are your specific plans to practice the discipline of secrecy this week? Do not share these plans with anyone, even an accountability partner. That could defeat the purpose of this discipline.

PART 2
disciplines of action

In the disciplines of abstinence, we do without something—food, talking, companionship, possessions, work, or recognition—in order to reap a spiritual benefit. In the disciplines of action, we *do* things—actions that bring us closer to God. In the normal course of one's spiritual life, the disciplines of abstinence and action are intertwined, but here we are studying them separately. The disciplines of action provide things we can do that open us to God's work. The disciplines featured in this book are journaling, hospitality, confession, Scripture, charity, prayer, and penance. Taking action in any of these areas does not make us holy, but these disciplines are a means of grace, an ordinary channel through which God's grace can flow to us. When we practice these disciplines, we put ourselves in the way of God's work, and he changes us.

7. journaling

Write down the revelation and make it plain on tablets.

—Habakkuk 2:2

Journaling is communing and communicating with God through writing. It is turning our thoughts into words and putting them down so we can face them squarely. It is talking with and listening to God without speaking. When journaling, we can pray, listen, study, worship, and confess. Journaling is a discipline that provides perspective on life and helps us adjust our priorities. Journaling is a path away from the emotional doldrums and depression that come from relying on feelings. Journaling moves our spiritual lives from the inner ear (where we hear God's quiet voice) through our hands (with which we write) to our eyes (with which we see). It makes communication with God more tangible. When God seems distant, it is time to journal, for this discipline brings our communication with him nearer.

the heritage of journaling

Journaling is a recent discipline though it has ancient roots. In the distant past, writing was reserved for the elite who had the time and money to pay for expensive ink, pens, and handmade paper. Average people did not write through most of history, so the discipline of journaling did not flourish until writing materials became inexpensive and the ability to write became common. For centuries the verbal disciplines of prayer, confession, and the recitation of Scripture formed the backbone of the spiritual life, along with other disciplines of action such as hospitality, charity, and penance. However, once writing became common, journaling flourished, even among secular people, and it emerged as a spiritual discipline. Perhaps we should say that it reemerged.

Journaling is in fact an ancient practice. When we read the book of Psalms, we are peeking into the personal journals of ancient followers of God. They complained to God, confessed their sins, grumbled about life, and cried out for deliverance. So while journaling is in some sense a recent discipline, it has ancient roots. When we read these ancient psalms, we yearn for similarly open and honest relationships with God. Perhaps we'll find that when we, too, start to journal. We might begin with the psalms themselves. After a preface on God's law at the beginning of the book, Psalms 3–7 illustrate how to journal prayers, praise, cries for deliverance, confession, and complaints to God. Then after a short break for two worship-journal psalms, we get four more wonderful examples of journaling in Psalms 10–13. If we would simply copy the first thirteen psalms, we would learn what it means to be honest with God in our own journaling. And we would still have 137 psalms left before having to write our own words!

time journaling

Perhaps the easiest point of entry into this discipline is keeping record of daily activities, time journals in which we record where we went and what we did. This accounting method of journaling simply chronicles our use of time in the same way that receipts track the money we have spent. Indeed, the practice of accounting itself is at the root of this style of journaling. We will one day be required to give an account to God for how we spent our time. By keeping time journals, we can review the past week's expenditures of time and adjust our plans for the coming week based on our priorities. What could be more natural than beginning a week with a daily planner? When we see before us the amount of time we actually spent the previous week in prayer, with our children, or serving others, we may discover that our priorities are out of whack. We can then adjust the coming week's schedule. Many busy people already keep time journals in the form of daily planners or electronic devices. But merely recording our use of time is not difficult; it is *reviewing* our time and modifying the coming week's schedule that takes discipline. It is easy to dismiss such journaling as elementary, yet John Wesley, one of the greatest journal keepers in modern times, kept what was like a time journal and allowed many rabbit-trail ideas to develop from it. There is another benefit to such a review. When we're feeling defeated and think we're not getting anything done, a review of the last week's time journal can be encouraging. We may realize that we've done plenty, that we've done some good things, and (considering the week's obligations) we've done pretty well. Reflecting on a time journal each week often brings us to praise God and thank him for his guidance and deliverance in the previous week. This sort of review prompts personal worship. Time journaling is the easiest way to start journaling. Many who practice this discipline reflect each Sunday or at the beginning of each month.

being honest with God

Journaling enables us to be honest with God by confessing who we really are. In journaling, we bring into the light our sins and desires—our deepest cravings, impure attitudes, darkest thoughts, and angry complaints against God. This is one reason many of the psalms take a sharp turn at the end. Once things are brought into the light, we get God's perspective on them. Journaling is a means of confession, being totally honest with God. Can we do that in our heads or under our breath? Sure. Such whispered confessions work just as well with God, but not with us. A written confession is so much more serious; it becomes more real to us than a mental confession does. So when we journal, we confess; we hide nothing from God. Of course, honestly confessing to God in writing means we have to keep our journals private. While God is not shocked at our deepest thoughts, others certainly would be.

being honest with ourselves

In a journal we come clean not only with God, but also with ourselves. We listen in on our own confessions. A journaled confession ends denial. It has a cleansing effect. It is freeing.

Journaling a confession leads not only to spiritual health, but also to psychological health. Honestly admitting to ourselves who we really are and what we are really thinking brings continuity to the soul; we become a more "together" person.

Coming clean with ourselves improves our relationships with others too. Consider a husband who confesses in his journal how he really feels about his wife's endless chatter each evening, in which she tells him every tiny detail of her day. In his journal, he confesses how bored he is, how he pretends to listen but doesn't hear a word, how tiresome it all is, and how he wishes she'd just let him sit and watch TV. But in confessing these things before God in absolute honesty, he discovers a new perspective—God's perspective. As he continues to write his complaint, he begins to shift direction. He reflects on how tired he is and how he's just trying to survive each day. Soon he is writing about how self-centered he can be. Before long, he admits that he ought to be interested at least in a brief report of his wife's day. By the time he has finished a second page in his journal, he is promising himself that he will turn off the TV and listen intently to her debriefing for ten minutes each day. Just ten minutes—no more, but it's a start. For this husband, journaling provided an occasion to be honest with himself, then see God's perspective. The journaling then influenced his relationships with others. (I suppose that the wife in the above story might make some discoveries in her journaling as well.)

journaling prayer

We can journal our prayers. Praying can be done silently in our heads or aloud in an audible voice. We can also pray in writing.

When we write our prayers, we give greater attention to the words. Journaled prayers often avoid the repetition that plagues verbal prayers. They are more to the point and more clearly defined. Journaled prayers can be reprayed over time, and they can be copied and sent to others for whom we are praying. And when they are answered, written prayers give us a chance to record and remember the victory. For most of us, journaling our prayers would be a doorway to a deeper and more powerful prayer life.

journaling Scripture

Scripture is another means of grace that combines well with journaling. The entry-level practice for journaling Scripture is simply to copy Scripture word-for-word into a journal. Even this simple act can be a powerful means of grace. When we copy Scripture, it goes through our minds in a different way than when we just read it. In the simple act of copying a passage, we often discover new insights. In copying the Psalms, we come to experience the feelings of the original writer. This recopying of another's journal can sometimes express our own thoughts even better than if we were to write them ourselves. But we can go further than copying Scriptures, though that is a good way to start. We can seek God's word *for us* from Scripture. This is called *devotional reading* of the Bible, searching for God's word to us today from a passage. When we do that, God speaks, usually by nudging us toward the personal application of the passage at hand. If we are journaling, we can write down that inner impression. By writing our thoughts, we can examine them more carefully to discern whether or not they truly are from

God. The written word is more easily scrutinized. Sometimes we cross out our first draft of what we thought God might be saying. When the guidance we receive from God is written down and carefully examined, it takes on far greater authority. If we feel sure that the words before us are truly God's words *to* us, they are hard to dismiss or ignore.

remembering and rejoicing

The greatest value of keeping a journal is the creation of a written record that we can use to remember what God has done. We humans easily forget past victories and answers to prayer. We can also forget the temptations we faced years ago and lose sympathy with others who are facing them today. We can come to believe that we have always been as good as we are right now and develop attitudes of pride and conceit. The Bible often calls God's children to *remember*, and journaling enables us to do that by providing a written record of God's work in our lives. The act of remembering was central to Jewish worship. The annual Passover celebration was a remembrance of the first Passover in Egypt. Most other feasts and fasts commemorated God's mighty acts in the past. When the Jews remembered God's faithfulness in the past, it increased their faith in him in the present and future. Likewise, the early Christians worshiped by remembering the resurrection—God's mightiest deed in history—and it brought them hope for the present and future. Hope for the future is rooted in the past. As we add to our journals year after year, we collect a potent testimony to God's mighty acts in our own lives. As we review each month, year, and decade what God has done, we can easily rejoice at his faithfulness. By doing so, we build our faith for the present and our hope for the future. Perhaps this is why people who journal seem so peaceful. They see today as a tiny slice of what God is doing over many generations, so they know from their own experience that God is faithful. They remember it because they have recorded it in their journals.

how to begin practicing journaling

decide how you will journal

Will you write by hand in a blank notebook, or will you keep a journal on your computer or in some other way? Which method would best fit your lifestyle? Some people journal sequentially, keeping a spiritual diary of sorts. Others journal by topic and organize their thoughts for reconsideration and later development. This is especially easy with computer journaling. Pick a method of journaling that best fits your style.

develop other journaling traditions

Consider developing a family Christmas journal in which each member publicly reflects (to the family) on the past year and sets goals for the coming year. Some churches journal, too, especially new ones. Often they rotate the responsibility for keeping the journal each week or month among the members, then review the journal as a group at a New Year's gathering or other service, rejoicing in God's work.

settle security issues

Never let another person have free access to your journal. Your honesty in your journal will be proportional to its security.

You can read aloud or copy sections for others, but never turn your journal loose for others to scan. If you use a blank book, find a place to store it that is completely secure. If you write your journal on a computer, protect the file by password. If you do an anonymous online blog, make sure you password protect it from others. Some great Christians of the past invented their own codes to encrypt their journals. Today, people can use free Internet programs to scramble their journals so they can be deciphered only with a keyword. John Wesley developed such an elaborate code for his private journals that it took two hundred years to break! However you do it, take care of security issues so you can be completely honest with God and yourself.

begin by copying Scripture

If you complain, "I'm not creative" or "I can't write," then start by simply copying Scripture, especially the book of Psalms. You may never move on—Psalms and other Scriptures may express everything you want to say in your journal. Why reinvent the wheel?

forget perfectionism

If you are the sort of person who frets over grammar, spelling, and neatness, determine to break that habit. God does not take off points for spelling errors.

doodle, draw, and diagram

Sometimes a picture is worth a thousand words. And a diagram can often clarify things better than text can. Leaving some open spaces on journal pages allows for later fill-in writing, after the thought has marinated for a few weeks. Women are more inclined to journal than are men because it is like keeping a diary. However, some men are better at visualizing ideas with drawings, charts, or pictures. These men can look at the visual items ten years later and still sort out the meaning. If you are a man, try journaling with drawings, sketches, and doodles to start.

avoid becoming spiritually morbid

If you are overly sensitive and too easily berate yourself for your shortcomings, make a rule that you will not write more than one negative thing per day in your journal. Journaling is intended to be a means of grace not a means of guilt. On the other hand, if you seldom feel guilty about anything at all, you might make a rule that you'll write at least one confession of weakness per journaling session. Journaling should be balanced.

vary the approach

Over time, develop a varied approach to the journaling methods outlined in this book. Try time journaling, confession journaling, prayer journaling, and Scripture journaling. Add other approaches as you think of them. Let your journal reflect who you are and who you are becoming. It is just between you and God.

decide where your journals go upon your death

Will you destroy your journals at some point in the future, or will you pass them on as a family heritage? Some people seal them up for a generation and release them to their grandchildren. Others make arrangements with a spouse to destroy or pass them on after their own death. You don't have to decide these matters immediately. But, like making a will, if you wait until you need to, it may be too late.

schedule periodic reflection times

When and how often would you schedule your reflecting times? Weekly? Monthly? Quarterly? Annually? Some Christians who journal take an annual retreat—a weekend alone with God—during which they review all their journals to date and celebrate God's great grace so far in their lives. When and where would you do such a thing?

what about you?

What are your specific plans to practice the discipline of journaling this week?

8. hospitality

Do not forget to entertain strangers, for by so doing some people have entertained angels without knowing it.

—Hebrews 13:2

Hospitality is opening our homes, hearts, and lives to others in order to develop loving relationships to the glory of God. The English word may sound too much like *hospital* or *hospice* for us to greet the discipline with delight. The Greek word brings out its biblical meaning better. It could be literally translated "lovers of strangers." Hospitality is inviting people we don't know into our personal space and making them feel at home. It is a friend-making skill. Practicing this discipline brings us wonderful new friends, and in the process, we become more interesting persons. In hospitality, we give and get friendship. When we learn this discipline well, it becomes an antidote to loneliness—our own and that of others.

friend making

Hospitality helps us develop friend-making skills. When we move, we discover how difficult it can be to break into the cliques at a new church. When that happens, we feel lonely. Or worse, the church may have no cliques! Some churches have no groupings of friends. People attend the services as they would a movie: watch the show and then go home. Churches can be lonely places sometimes. Hospitality practiced in a church helps people make friends. Although the inviting may be done by just one person, well-practiced hospitality will spread throughout the congregation and have massive social consequences. Though the Bible commends hospitality and even commands that we show it to others, those who practice hospitality get something out of it too: friends. Hospitality teaches us how to make friends, a skill we need more as we get older. People who have automatic friendships because they still live near childhood friends and family sometimes rarely learn the skill of making friends. As their friends move away or die, these people are increasingly left alone and friendless in the world. They *had* friends but never *made* them. Learning the discipline of friend making enables us to move a thousand miles away or enter a nursing home far from family and not be lonely. We can always have friends because we know how to make them. We should practice hospitality because it is right and good, even if we get nothing out of it. But it does produce a significant personal benefit—friends.

the spiritual discipline of hospitality

Although hospitality brings friendship, this chapter is not about making friends or even the discipline of practicing hospitality. It is about the *spiritual* discipline of hospitality. What makes hospitality spiritual? For starters, hospitality is commanded in the Bible. Indeed all of the great religions of the world insist on this virtue. (The fact that some other religions practice it better than Christians do should discomfort us.) But anyone can show hospitality. It becomes a spiritual discipline—a Christian discipline—when we do it for Christ and the kingdom of God, not just to have a good time with our friends after church. Just as dieting is not fasting, so entertaining is not necessarily hospitality. Our motives are the test. Why do we invite others over, and who do we invite? Our motives will reveal whether or not we are practicing true Christian hospitality. The spiritual discipline of hospitality is not just having fun with friends, but also includes inviting strangers. Hospitality adds an invitation to people who are not in one's clique. Hospitality reaches out to bring strangers into the inner circle. Hospitality is thus a selfless act. It is done for the other person, stranger, lonely person, new person, and person who doesn't fit in. Hospitality is unselfish, which is why it is a *spiritual* discipline and why it is rare. It becomes a means of grace as God works through the relationships hospitality enables. God favors working through groups. This is why he left us with a command to gather together instead of a command to engage in the solitary life. While many of the disciplines in this book are solitary, they are not intended to produce a solitary lifestyle. They should lead us back into the church, where most of God's sanctifying work is done. When we practice hospitality, we connect with others. God speaks *to* us through them and *through* us to them. Hospitality is a discipline because it is not natural. We naturally invite our friends to our homes; we also supernaturally invite strangers.

hospitality in the Bible

The Bible frequently gives examples of hospitality. Abraham opened his tent to strangers. Jesus was born after his parents were offered hospitality. Mary and Martha offered their home to Jesus on his visits to Jerusalem. In fact, hospitality was universally considered a virtue in the ancient world where desert travel could mean death if local people did not open their homes to strangers. But this practice is not merely an ancient custom designed for eras without rest stops or motels. It is a virtue we ought to practice today. Paul told the Romans to "practice hospitality" (Rom. 12:13). The writer of Hebrews reminds us that by showing hospitality to strangers, "some people have entertained angels without knowing it" (Heb. 13:2). Peter said we are to "offer hospitality to one another without grumbling" (1 Pet. 4:9). John instructed us on how to treat itinerant speakers: "Show hospitality to such men" (3 John 8). The early church considered hospitality compulsory for widows called to church work (1 Tim. 5:9–10) and for church leaders, too, including bishops and overseers (1 Tim. 3:2; Titus 1:7–8). Perhaps the most startling teaching on hospitality comes from the mouth of Jesus. He taught that on the day of judgment, some of us will be condemned for our lack of hospitality to him only to discover that by failing to show hospitality to strangers, we have rejected Jesus himself (Matt. 25:34–40). This is not to suggest a hospitality-or-hell doctrine, but we certainly cannot ignore Jesus' teaching on this point. Hospitality is not merely a nice thing to do; it may be introduced as evidence at the judgment.

reasons we resist

Why are we so slow to invite people outside of our social group into our homes? How come so many of us go for weeks without opening our homes to anyone at all, let alone strangers? To start with, we are busy. Many of us live at such a frantic pace that we don't have the time to practice hospitality. We might arrange for a quick meal at a restaurant or an evening at the movies, but we simply don't have time to invite people into our homes. There is another reason though. If we invite our friends or our small group over and add a few newcomers to the mix, our friends may wonder, "What are *they* doing here?" Most of us like stable cliques or small groups, so if we let our natural selves rule, we will fellowship only with those we already know and like. Inviting strangers into our groups may make our friends feel awkward, so we don't even try.

hospitality versus entertainment

If we feel compelled to do something elaborate whenever people come to our homes, we may not be practicing true hospitality. Rushing home to clean the house and arrange an impressive meal could indicate that we are more concerned about impressing people than in being hospitable. Hospitality is about the guest, not the host. It does not focus on the host's skill at making fancy preparation or immaculate housekeeping, but on answering this question: What will make people feel a part of our family? Being a fancy host who elaborately entertains can merely be a way to gather an audience for oneself. Hospitality is inviting. It invites people in not to become an audience, but to experience family life. The best hospitality makes strangers feel at home. It makes guests want to kick off their shoes and put on slippers.

our example

God is the original host, of course. He extended an invitation to us when we were strangers—even enemies—to come into his family. He desires a relationship with us and calls us to himself. God is the shepherd-host who prepares a table before us. At his final meal on earth, the Last Supper, Jesus promised that we would one day join him at another meal—the marriage supper of the Lamb. God has invited us into the warmth of his family. Now he asks us to do likewise, inviting others into our homes. God is hospitable. Hospitality is godly. Practicing the discipline of hospitality makes us more like God.

men and hospitality

Hospitality is sometimes wrongly considered a feminine virtue. Men are not exempt from the call to hospitality. A man's personal space might be the garage, yard, or hunting lodge, but men can still be inviting of strangers. Men practice hospitality when they call a neighbor to their garage to help unload the lawn mower rather than insisting on doing it themselves. When men invite a couple of strangers along with their friends to watch the game, they are practicing hospitality. Men practice hospitality when they invite an outsider to join their buddies on the annual hunting trip. Hospitality opens one's personal space and life to other people, especially strangers, in order to develop relationships with them. Men should do this just as much as women should. Some just do it differently.

third-step hospitality

The first step in hospitality is inviting friends into our personal spaces. But what credit is it that we show hospitality to the people we like? Not much—this is the sort of things even pagans do. It is not wrong to invite friends over, but it is not the spiritual discipline of hospitality. If we need discipline to spend time with our friends, we probably need therapy! The spiritual discipline of hospitality goes a second step: inviting strangers, outsiders, foreigners, and outcasts into our lives. This is why it is a *discipline*; it isn't normal behavior for self-centered people and self-protecting cliques to reach out to strangers. So second-step hospitality is inviting strangers along with friends.

However, there is a third step to hospitality. Third-step hospitality is inviting *enemies* into our lives. This step brings an enemy into one's personal space in order to build or heal a relationship. It is hard to eat with an enemy. Either an enemy will destroy the meal, or the meal will destroy the enemy. Christians destroy their enemies by making them friends. Eating together melts icy relationships, heals hurting wounds, and cures smoldering anger. Either that will happen, or the person will walk away. Hospitality forces a resolution. Eating together is sacred, perhaps even a means of grace when taken as such. That may be one reason Jesus established a communal meal, the Eucharist, as a tangible reminder of his death and the core element of worship. Eating brings people together.

So are we ready for third-step hospitality: inviting an enemy for dinner? Could we invite some people who are estranged from church to the next party? They could say no, of course. But the discipline of hospitality is not about what *they* do. It is about what *we* do. Most of Christ's church needs to move toward second-step hospitality—inviting strangers along with friends. And a few of us should feel compelled to go the third step: showing hospitality to our enemies.

communal hospitality

This book focuses on personal disciplines, but we should at least be aware that there is such a thing as *communal hospitality*. A group can be either hospitable or inhospitable, just like an individual. Hospitality for a church is making room for outsiders and turning them into insiders. Some churches are simply inhospitable places. They claim, "We're a loving church, just like a family." What they don't add is, "In fact, this church *is* a family and nobody else can break into our close-knit circle!" It is possible for a church to be a loving place for the people already in the club and be inhospitable to outsiders. When we practice hospitality as a church, we warmly welcome newcomers. We scoot down the pew to make room for visitors so they don't have to climb over us to find a seat. We encourage new people to lead a discussion in Sunday school or serve as ushers. Hospitable churches make newcomers feel at home. And the newcomers stay because after just a few weeks, they consider the new church to be their home. All churches get rid of strangers. Inhospitable churches get rid of strangers by cold-shouldering them away; hospitable churches get rid of them by making them friends. When we practice hospitality at church, we are being like God because he invited us into his family when we were his enemies. Of all places, the church should be the most hospitable.

how to begin practicing hospitality

offer a guest room to the church

Offer the guest room in your home to guest speakers or college groups that might need a place to stay when coming to your church. The use of motel lodging for speakers is a great time saver for the church, but it often banishes the speaker to a lonely life in a sterile atmosphere. Inviting a guest into your home will enrich your life, and if you have children, it will immensely affect their future. Don't entertain your guests to death or dump your problems on them. In fact, don't even spend too much time picking their brains for a good idea. Let them rest just as they would at their own home—this is hospitality.

feed the birds

OK, it sounds silly. But perhaps hospitality could begin by feeding the birds or even those bothersome squirrels in your neighborhood. If you're the kind of person who'd rather shoot animals than welcome them, perhaps that attitude bleeds over into your relationships with people. If so, learn to be more welcoming to the animal trespassers at your home, and you may become more welcoming to the human interlopers in your life. If you start with the birds, you can move up to people later!

invite neighbors over some night this week

How long have you lived where you now live? Have you had your neighbors into your home yet? Have you invited them for a meal? Invite one neighbor this week, not for a whole evening with fancy fixings; just order a pizza and get to know them. At least get them inside your home.

open your home to the youth group

Youth groups are always looking for new places to go. Offer your house, yard, or barn to the youth leaders in your church, and decide ahead of time that you won't walk around and do damage assessment when they leave.

invite a single or married person to your home

If you are married, invite a single person to your home. If single, invite a married couple. Find someone whose family situation is different from yours and include them in what you are doing. Who knows? Maybe you'll make a new friend.

add someone to your holiday invitation list

Can you think of anyone who might be alone this Thanksgiving or Christmas? Why not invite them to join you for the holiday? You wouldn't lose much, and they would gain a ton. If you were to do this, who would you invite?

what about you?

What are your specific plans to practice the discipline of hospitality this week?

9. confession

Therefore confess your sins to each other and pray for
each other so that you may be healed. The prayer
of a righteous man is powerful and effective.

—James 5:16

The spiritual discipline of confession is humbly admitting our
sins and shortcomings to another person as a means of spiritual
healing. Of course we should confess first to God in prayer. But
the spiritual discipline of confession is not about confessing to God
in solitude but about confessing to another person in community.
Confession is good for the soul. The act of confessing is humbling.
It prevents us from casting an image that is better than we really
are. Confessing our sins to one another lets others see through us.
In confession, we become transparent. We make known to others
what God already knows. Of course, another person cannot forgive
our sins; only God can do that. But another person who serves as
a confessor can represent God in affirming that we are indeed
forgiven. Thus, confession can bring assurance of forgiveness to

us. There is no stronger vice than a hidden one. Confessing our sins and temptations before another person weakens sin's hold on us. While most of the other spiritual disciplines are conducted in private, this one requires another person. Confession is an interpersonal spiritual discipline that produces significant personal gains. It produces enormous psychological benefits as well.

desire for privacy

Why not keep our sins and faults just between God and us? Why get others involved? Nobody can forgive sins but God—there is only one mediator between God and mankind, Christ Jesus. But the Bible calls us to go beyond private confession to God alone, saying, "Confess your sins to each other" (James 5:16). What right do we have to dismiss this command? Christians are supposed to find other Christians and make full confessions to them. This is biblical. Certainly, we ought to confess to God first, but then we should finish the work by finding another person or small group with whom to complete our confessions. Why is this so hard to obey? Perhaps it is because of the second half of a well-known quote: "Confession is good for the soul . . . but bad for the reputation." The point of the quote is to remind us that keeping our confession between God and us is safer in terms of our reputations with others. Confessing to others would give those people a glimpse of who we really are. It could harm our carefully manicured reputation. That is why confession is the most powerful antidote to the nastiest sin of all—pride. We don't have to confess everything to everybody, but we certainly ought to confess *some* things to someone. The Bible tells us to.

benefits of confession

The fact that the Bible commands confession should be reason enough for us to do it, but there are benefits beyond obedience. Confession is a humbling experience, so when we do it, we increase the virtue of humility within ourselves. Confession opens the door to feeling forgiven. We may have long ago confessed our sins to God yet still feel a tinge of guilt. Why? Because *being* forgiven and *feeling* forgiven are two different things. We can be forgiven in a moment by God yet continually carry a sense of guilt. When we confess to others, see their forgiving attitude, and hear their pronouncement that God has indeed forgiven us, we often find the assurance of forgiveness that we crave. Feeling forgiven makes it easier to forgive ourselves.

Confession also provides accountability. Each of us will someday give an account of ourselves before God. Confession lets us make an accounting before a confidant here on earth. When we have confessed our sins and temptations to others, we give them permission to correct and caution us. Confession connects us with other people and makes our temptations and sins their business too. It gives them permission to watch, nudge, remind, and even reprove us.

The greatest benefit of confession may be the healing power we receive from doing it. Confession has a curative effect. This is why James finished his statement about confession with a word about healing. He said, "Confess your sins to each other and pray for each other *so that you may be healed*" (James 5:16, emphasis added). There is both physical and spiritual healing in owning up to our sins and temptations. It heals our wounds. It makes us better and stronger. It helps us recover. This curative effect of confession is central to all twelve-step recovery programs. In step four, people make "a searching and fearless moral inventory" of their lives, confessing their true states. A chain of addictive behavior is often connected to hidden past resentments. There is healing and freedom in bringing others into the quiet sanctuary of our lives, making a full confession to them, then receiving their affirmation that God has indeed completely forgiven us.

confession in the early church

This spiritual discipline is a hard one for Protestants to accept. We conjure images of Catholics lined up at the confessional where priests wait to dispense forgiveness. We complain, "But only God can forgive sins!" We would rather keep our sins between God and us, naturally. So while we recognize that the Bible urges us to confess, we are slow to obey. But our mental images of confession only show our ignorance of Christian history. For one thing, even in the Roman Catholic Church, priests do not dispense forgiveness. Also, confession was never a strictly Catholic rite. Confession as a ritual appeared fairly early in the church and took its place in weekly worship long before the emergence of the Roman church. Actually, at the very beginning, the church had no provision whatsoever for dealing with sin after a person was baptized; it was simply assumed that sin was gone forever once a person entered the kingdom of God. Experience taught otherwise, however. The church rapidly responded with two rituals that dealt with sin after baptism: confession and penance. Making confession a ritual (as opposed to a spiritual discipline) is not without problems. It is easy to get on the sin-and-confess treadmill. The Christian life hopes for more than a weekly emptying of the trash on Sunday. Penance was added to confession by the fourth century so that a person would have to do more than simply confess sin and walk away. Penance was supposed to train people to stop sinning. Eventually, the church specified precise acts of penance for certain sins, just as the laws of every country in the world now do. So confession has been a part of the church from its early stages.

Luther and Calvin

Through the Middle Ages, confession was corrupted and even used in fund-raising schemes along with other rites and sacraments of the church. In the 1500s, the Reformer Martin Luther rejected the idea that a person was required to make confession to a priest, but Luther was deeply convinced that making confession to a priest was a means of grace for believers. The Protestants, as those who accepted the Reformers' ideas became known, believed that all believers are priests and it was therefore possible to make confession to any other believer. The "priesthood of believers" did *not* mean that a person could serve as his or her own priest, as many assume now. It meant that any other believer—not just a member of the clergy—could serve as a priest and hear confessions. John Calvin, another Reformer, also opposed compulsory confession but valued private confession because he saw how it brought assurance of sins forgiven. However, Calvin preferred that pastors serve as the confessors for the people.

John Wesley and confession

Because John Wesley is well-known for his teaching on sanctification and holiness, one might think he'd have little to say about confession. What would a holy people confess? However, the opposite is true of John Wesley. In the 1700s, he took this spiritual discipline more seriously than any Protestant before and perhaps since. In weekly small-group sessions called class meetings, the Methodists were instructed to speak freely and plainly about the true state of their souls. While Wesley taught the possibility of living a holy life, he did not ignore the need for confession. In his meetings, four questions of accountability were to be asked of each person every week: What known sins have you committed since our last meeting? What temptations have you met with? How were you delivered? What have you thought, said, or done of which you doubt whether it be sin or not?

Do you know of many Christians today—even Wesley's heirs, those in the Holiness Movement—who risk facing such questions among their peers each week? While some cell groups and accountability groups take confession as seriously as Wesley did, it is rare. Imagine going around the circle one by one in a small group confessing every sin you are aware of committing since the last meeting. If you have not knowingly sinned, certainly you have been tempted, so you would talk about those temptations and precisely how you were delivered from sinning. Finally, you would submit to the group's spiritual leaders by reporting anything you have thought, said, or done of which you're unsure whether is sin or not; then the group would help decide if it was sin (moderating the too-sensitive conscience or the seared conscience).

Most of us who live in a world where spirituality has been privatized and secretized cannot imagine following John Wesley's approach. We say, "It's none of their business!" or, "That's between me and God." Most of us would be terrified of doing this sort of confession with a group of people. But could we do it with one person?

confession and us

Martin Luther, John Calvin, and John Wesley were then; this is now. They were themselves, and we need to be ourselves. So do *we* need confession now? If so, how? Certainly a counseling setting provides a good format for some confession. In fact, pastoral counseling and friendship counseling may be the dominant settings in which we confess today. Many Protestants don't know that the traditional confession booth of the Roman Catholic Church has largely been replaced by what is now called the sacrament of reconciliation, something more like face-to-face therapeutic counseling than the veiled confessional we see in movies. But still, fewer Catholics today confess by either mode. And very few Protestants confess at any time.

Could it be that we take confession less seriously today because we now take sin less seriously? Yet God takes sin seriously, and we should too. So we should confess—both to God and to someone else. Some worship liturgies include a generic, weekly confession in which we admit as a group, "We have done things we ought not to have done and left things undone we ought to have done." That helps, and may open us up to practicing personal confession more consistently. But the practice of specific and personal confession is rare outside of a scattering of accountability groups and small groups. Perhaps it is time to restore confession to Protestant circles. Then we'd see more of the humility, release, healing, and liberation it supplies.

what to confess

There is more to confess than sin. We have spoken mostly of confessing sin but there is much more to confess to your confidant or confessor when you get one. Here are some things to confess.

recent purposeful sin

Sin is like a fire in that it can be quenched at first with a glass of water, but left to itself, it will consume the whole house. Confessing recent sin cuts a firebreak across the path of spreading sin.

recent unintentional sin

Even if our intentions are perfect, we sometimes sin against one another and don't know it until it is pointed out. We become accountable for these sins once we know about them, and they should be confessed. Often, sins of the tongue are in this category.

sins of attitude

Inner attitudes in the recesses of our hearts like bitterness, grudges, ill will, envy, racism, jealousy, or resentment should be confessed.

recent temptations

What sin is Satan enticing us toward? What sinful attitudes could grow if we don't weaken their hold by bringing them into the light?

past sins

Even if they are long-ago forgiven, if we still sense some level of guilt for past sins, we may need to confess them to bring final inner healing.

flaws and faults

Even though they are not sins, flaws and faults can still block our spiritual effectiveness. So we confess things like being too self-centered, talking too much, being too easily hurt, being lazy, being overly sensitive, saying harsh words, or other tendencies that could lead to sin or make us less effective.

Can we imagine what regular confession of this sort would do for us? Think of the change that would come over a church body that did what we are all supposed to do—confess sins one to another. Why do we linger and delay? This would be a great week to start the discipline of confession and get in the flow of God's grace through this channel.

how to begin practicing confession

confess something this week to someone

Even if you do not take this chapter very seriously, at least confess one thing to someone this week, even if you consider it only homework for this book. Come clean about one thing to a coworker, friend, or spouse. Perhaps you aren't attracted to high-grade confession, but you could do something low-grade couldn't you? Do you feel you have nothing to confess? Then ask your roommate, spouse, or children for suggestions.

be careful of broadcasting confessions

Sensing full forgiveness from others sometimes leads an immature person to confess too broadly. Confession is not advertising. It is not designed to tell everybody your tawdry sins in order to give them something to talk about. It is for you so you can be humbled and assured of God's grace and forgiveness. The circle of confession seldom needs to be larger than the circle of offense.

think of someone who could become a personal confessor

Who would you go to if you wanted to confess something? Who could you trust to keep things secret? Who would have the grace to hear your confession forgivingly? Who would have the wisdom to guide you and the authority to assure you that God has indeed (perhaps long ago) forgiven you on the basis of the death of Jesus Christ? Can you think of such a person? Would it be a pastor or layperson? Someone near or far away? Someone you already know or a stranger you've heard about? If you are to begin this discipline, you will need someone who you can confess to. The first step is thinking of who that might be.

talk with your prospective confessor

When you find a person whom you would like to confide in, tell that person what you want to do. Show this chapter to the person and ask if he or she is willing to hear your confession and assure you of God's grace.

start small

Although you may trust your confidant or confessor, start small. Review the list above, and start with your flaws and faults before working up to recent sin. Don't worry; as you find the joy of true confession, you'll be motivated to move deeper on the list.

accept God's word through your confessor

Just as you allow God to speak to you through your preacher, let him speak through your confessor. This is the best understanding of the concept of the priesthood of all believers. Listen for God's assurance that you are forgiven, and believe it. You may have to help your confessor understand that you aren't looking for advice so much as assurance. Good advisors are often poor confessors. What you need is a listening ear, an accepting smile, a gentle spirit, a nodding head, kind eyes, empathetic facial gestures, and a person who will speak God's words into your life and then pray without giving you advice.

what about you?

What are your specific plans to practice the discipline of confession this week?

10. scripture

*All Scripture is God-breathed and is useful for teaching,
rebuking, correcting and training in righteousness.*

—2 Timothy 3:16

Scripture as a spiritual discipline is <u>reading, studying,</u>
<u>memorizing, meditating upon, and obeying the Bible in order to</u>
<u>know God and become more like him.</u> Scripture is perhaps the
primary personal spiritual discipline in use today and is usually
practiced by means of the modern habit of having personal
devotions, where it is combined with prayer. Scripture is not the
oldest spiritual discipline (prayer has been around much longer),
but since the Reformation, it has become the most important
one for Protestants. In Scripture, we find the story of God and
his people. Here we discover God's values, commands, and
character, and we discover what he expects from us. The Bible
was not given primarily to tell us how to live, but to show us
who God is, because once we truly know who he is, we will

know how to live. While the Bible demands a particular lifestyle, Scripture is more than a collection of rules. It is the story of God; he is the primary subject of the Bible. It is his story.

the word in the Word

The very best way to get to know God is to get to know Jesus. Jesus is the revelation of God; he came to show us who God is. Thus, we Christians should especially focus our attention on the four gospels, for there we find God in Christ Jesus. God did not send the Bible to die for our sins; he sent his Son, Jesus. We do not worship the Bible but Jesus Christ. The Word of God is Christ, but the Bible is our record of this Word. The Bible is precious to us. How would we know of Jesus Christ if we had no Scripture? All of Scripture is inspired — Leviticus, Ezra, Hebrews, and Jude, along with the Gospels, where we find the revelation of God, Jesus. Thus, we read the whole Bible, not just the Gospels. But as Christians (and as the Christian church), we make the Gospels central to our reading because the incarnation, life, death, and resurrection of Jesus Christ the Son of God are central to our faith. This is why we call ourselves *Christ*ians.

how Scripture changes us

Words are powerful. They can cause people to like or hate us. They can incite persecution, racism, violence, or war. They can also rouse compassion, tenderness, or understanding and bring peace. The capacity to use words may be the most powerful capability God has granted to us. Perhaps he did so because we are created in his own image. Used properly, words can be used by parents to send their children in the right direction in life.

Used wrongly, words can cause wounds from which children may spend their lifetimes recovering. Words are pilgrims as they pass through our ears but become permanent settlers in our heads and hearts. If our own human words have this much power, imagine the power of God's words. As God's words pass through our ears and take residence inside us, we are changed. Over time we become what we see, hear, and say. When we practice the spiritual discipline of Scripture, we begin to think like God. We come to adopt God's values and begin living toward his ideals. These changes often occur quietly and slowly, but they do happen. A daughter who constantly hears her father affirm her preciousness develops a strong sense of self-worth. What goes in comes out. As we get into the Word, it gets into us, and we are transformed by it. We become more like God. It molds us into an image of his Son, Jesus Christ. Thus, Scripture is usually our chief discipline for personal spiritual formation. It has the power to change who we are, how we think, and how we live. Scripture changes us when it gets inside us. So what are the ways we get Scripture inside us?

devotional reading

By far the most common means of absorbing Scripture is devotional reading, reading the Bible to hear what God has to say through it to us. Devotional reading of Scripture is more than reading a devotional book. It is reading Scripture devotionally. This kind of reading can be perilous, of course, for we could easily read our own desires into just about any verse. Through all of history, from the early desert fathers to today, believers have read the Bible this way. God has chosen to meet his people in the words of the Bible. God does indeed "speak" to us personally by using texts that meant something quite different than when they were first written. Bible scholars tremble when non-scholar Christians announce that God used a certain verse to tell them to accept a new job they've been praying about. Bible scholars mutter under their breath, "That verse is about the nation of Israel, not your new job. It was written to a group of people over two thousand years ago about their future, not to you personally about your career!" But non-scholar believers are unconvinced. They accept that the Bible had an original meaning and was written to an original audience, yet they still believe God speaks to them personally about very different matters through those same words.

This is devotional reading. It is using the Bible to hear a personal word from God. Could God take a verse that was originally directed to one rich man long ago and use that verse to tell St. Anthony to sell all his possessions and follow Jesus full time? Well, he did. Most Christians would agree that God speaks this way through the Bible. A devotional interpretation does not apply to all people at all times, but it can apply to one person here and now. When we read the Bible this way, we are really using it as a sort of prayer mechanism, a way to listen for God's voice through Scripture. It is the most popular way we use the Bible today. When we practice devotional reading, we are really listening to the Holy Spirit, who in turn uses the words of Scripture to speak to us. The Spirit could use a dictionary if he wanted to, but we are more likely to hear his prompting rightly through Scripture than from a dictionary. Devotional reading has its limitations and dangers, but it becomes far less dangerous if we also study the Scriptures.

study

Bible study is a serious effort to discover what the Bible meant when it was written and then to draw out what it means for us today. Study takes us into the text to discover what the words meant to the original audience and how the words would have been heard when the Bible was written. Once we've discovered what the verses meant when they were written, we then can move to apply that truth to today's world. Study can become a leash on our devotional interpretations of Scripture, reining them in and making them conform to the meaning of the whole Bible. In study, we often employ additional resources like study Bibles, commentaries, and other books. Study takes us into the world of the patriarchs before there was a Bible or the Ten Commandments. It lets us visit ancient Israel and makes the psalms spring alive before us. Study enables us to travel through time to the first century and see how women and children were treated in those days so we can make sense of the Bible's instructions for women in worship.

memorization

There was a time when memorizing Scripture was more prevalent than it is today. Many Christians now can't imagine that for the first fifteen hundred years of Christian history (and throughout the Old Testament period), printed Bibles were rare or unavailable. Until modern times, the only Bible average Christians had was what they heard read aloud on Sundays or had committed to memory. There were no Bibles sitting on end tables or stacked neatly in pew racks. (There weren't even seats in churches for most of that time; people stood.) For hundreds of years, most Christians didn't have the luxury of taking a break from their work to read a few verses from their pocket New Testament or on their smartphones. It is no wonder they went to church more often and memorized Scripture. It is rare today for Christians to make serious attempts to memorize Scripture, and we have lost something by abandoning that discipline. We no longer have Scripture on the tips of our tongues or in our heads. We no longer know where a verse is located. Instead, we say, "Somewhere in the Bible it says . . ." and then quote Benjamin Franklin's almanac and not actual Scripture. The greatest loss we suffer from our failure to memorize Scripture is the absence of a mental library of verses to meditate and ponder on throughout the day. Memorizing Scripture builds our library one verse at a time. Then we can retrieve, contemplate, and apply it to life situations as we face them. When we have few verses memorized, we relegate Scripture to a few corners of life, such as morning devotions or church. When tempted in the wilderness, Jesus was able to quote specific Scriptures related to each temptation. Memorizing Scripture prepares us to resist the Devil. It changes us. That, of course, is what we really mean when we say that we've learned a Scripture "by heart."

meditation

Meditation is turning Scripture over in our minds, pondering it slowly. This is often done after we've memorized a passage, but it can also be done as a means of reading Scripture. It is slowly digesting the words, quietly ruminating on them, and reverentially allowing them to soak into the consciousness. This sort of reading is sometimes called *lectio divina* (divine reading) and is often seen as a means of finding union with God. When we meditate on Scripture, we let the words marinate in our minds and seep deeply into our hearts. As we do this, fresh truth emerges and clearer direction comes from God. We do not have to know much Scripture to begin meditating; almost all Christians already know the Lord's Prayer, John 3:16, and at least some of Psalm 23. With these few verses, we can begin the practice of meditation as we drive our cars, ride in elevators, or check the mailbox. While Eastern religions sometimes train their followers to meditate as a means of clearing the mind to arrive at complete emptiness, Christian meditation aims to fill the mind—with Scripture. As we do this, God's values gradually displace our own, and we start thinking more like him. This is the power of Scripture and from it, we gain the mind of God.

hearing the Word

The Scriptures were not originally intended for silent reading. They were meant to be read aloud, to be heard. Today, we engage Scripture with our eyes. Throughout most of Christian history, Scripture did not enter people's minds through their eyes, but through their ears. This is why early church leaders were urged to give themselves to the public reading of Scripture; that's how people gained access to God's Word. In fact, most of the New Testament was not written to any individual; it was addressed to a group and was meant to be read to the entire gathered church. Hearing Scripture is different from seeing it. The ear detects different nuances in the Bible. Hearing Scripture changes how we perceive it. We hear some Scripture readings at church, so long as we don't open the pew Bible and read along, but we can experience this transformational listening at home or in the car by means of sound recordings or read the Bible aloud to ourselves and hear the shift in meaning as we listen to Scripture even in our own voices. When reading Scripture aloud, we automatically interpret it by our tones, inflections, and styles of reading. Even if we listen to recorded Scriptures and zone out after several chapters, the words still affect us even when we think we're not listening. Isn't that what we tell teenagers about their music? Sure, active listening is better, but even passive listening can change a person.

doing the Word

Our objective is more than reading, study, memorizing, and meditating on the Word; it is *living* the Word that we are after. The Bible was not given for our information but for our transformation. To Protestants, the Bible is almost a sacrament, a God-ordained place where he chooses to meet with and transform his people—a primary means of grace. When we come under its influence, Scripture makes us into something new and different and more like Christ. Perhaps the reason we are not enough like Christ is that too few of us make the Bible prominent in our lives. The spiritual discipline of Scripture gets us into the stream where God is moving so that we might be healed, becoming whole and transforming into the image of his Son, Jesus Christ.

how to begin practicing Scripture

spread out your Bibles

How many Bibles do you own? Two? Five? Seven? Distribute them around your work and living areas: one in the living room, another in the bedroom, one in the office by the computer, another in the car, and so on. There's no use piling them all in one place. Make them accessible, then watch how the Holy Spirit will prompt you to pick up a Bible and read it from time to time.

start where you are

What are you already doing with Scripture? List the ways in which you already practice this discipline, and don't be discouraged if you fall short of the ideal. You have to start somewhere. For example, make a list of how many verses you already have memorized: the Lord's Prayer, perhaps, and some others. Start with what you know.

begin having daily devotions

If you've been thinking about doing this for years but never started, this week would be a good time to begin. Or more likely, you might have a sporadic practice of personal Bible reading and prayer, so this week would be a great time to begin daily devotions, even if you do it for only ten minutes at a time. Setting a devotional goal too high defeats many well-intentioned Christians. Set reachable goals that could reasonably be continued throughout your life, and don't increase them for months, maybe even years. The other disciplines in this book will take up some of your time too; there's more to do besides reading Scripture. Sure you could go full steam ahead with all these disciplines, but then you'd have no time for work, family, or even sleep. So start carefully and go for consistency, not discipline-mania. Do something this week and do it every day. Start small.

listen to Scripture

If you were attracted to the notion of listening to the Scriptures, order, borrow, or download one of the many inexpensive Scripture recordings that are available. If you especially enjoy music, consider buying a recording of Scriptures sung or recorded with musical accompaniment. Put them in your car, near your CD player, or on your smartphone and decide what sort of habit you'll create in order to listen regularly, like playing them every Sunday morning as you're getting ready for church or on Wednesdays during your commute to work. You'll love how this soothes and transforms your spirit. And it's easy.

journal Scripture

Simply start copying portions of Scripture in your own handwriting—slowly and thoughtfully, with reverence, as the scribes and monks once did. This may seem silly at first. After all, with modern printing presses and computer programs, you could just print out the verses, but stay with it. Watch what happens to you by the time you've done half of one book of the Bible. People who journal Scripture perhaps know best of all the transforming power of these words. Writing by hand slows down the usually rushed pace at which you consume Scripture and forces you to meditate on the words as you write. If you have an artistic flair, you may find yourself drawing doodles or other pictures alongside the text—exactly as many monks did in the past. If you've never done this, it may sound strange. But give it a try and see how transforming it may be for you, even when you copy familiar texts.

set a study time

To avoid the trap of spending 100 percent of Bible time in devotional reading, set a time when you'll seriously study the Word. What would you set as a balanced schedule to blend both devotional reading and Bible study? A 100-percent-study type person needs to add more devotional reading. A 100-percent-devotional reader needs to upgrade the amount of study. Most mature Christians would say a balanced approach to both devotional reading and study is best.

start a memorization plan

With a partner, start a plan for memorizing Scripture so you can meditate on it. Be careful to avoid making this a race, as if the goal is simply to memorize a greater number of verses. Instead, measure your success at memory work by the number of verses you implement in your life. The goal of Scripture memorization is not learning but living.

what about you?

What are your specific plans to practice the discipline of Scripture this week?

11. charity

*For I was hungry and you gave me something to eat, I was thirsty
and you gave me something to drink, I was a stranger and you
invited me in, I needed clothes and you clothed me, I was sick and
you looked after me, I was in prison and you came to visit me.*

—Matthew 25:35–36

Charity is giving aid to the poor and is motivated by a selfless
love. It is love in action, sometimes known as the biblical virtue
of lovingkindness. While an organization dedicated to helping
the poor may be called a charity, charity is a personal discipline
as well. It is both central to the Christian faith and evidence of
it. This spiritual discipline is not merely an attitude of pity or a
feeling of love, but an action that helps. In the Bible, charity is
referred to as almsgiving, and it was simply expected of the
Israelites and Jesus' disciples. James the brother of Jesus considered
charity a test of pure religion, evidence that we are indeed
followers of God. This discipline changes the lives of both
the poor and those who practice it. When we practice charity,
we find fulfillment as God uses our hands to do his work in the

world. We take up Christ's work, becoming his hands and feet, his gift to the poor.

God's concern for the poor

"God must especially love the poor because he made so many of them." This wisecrack is only half right. God does love the poor, but it is not God who made them poor. Why does he care so much about the poor? Because of who he is: a God of compassion. Christ illustrated this. He came to earth primarily as a savior not a healer, yet the Gospels report scores of healings. Why? Why didn't Jesus simply get on with his Father's business of preaching the truth and dying for our sins? Jesus healed precisely because he *was* doing his Father's business. Jesus inaugurated his earthly mission by proclaiming that his goal was to help the poor (Luke 4:18–19), and he named healing as evidence of his true identity when questioned about it by John the Baptist (Luke 7:22). Christ showed his compassion for people in need. By doing so, he was showing us what God is like. Jesus Christ is God-in-action. God cares for the poor. So we might ask, "If he cares so much about the poor, why doesn't he send angels to help them?" The answer is that he has. He has sent us.

the undeserving poor

We who are well-off sometimes wonder if the poor are victims of their own laziness and lack of motivation. We are tempted to think that the poor are poor because they don't have the gumption to scramble their way up the ladder as we have and as our parents did. We think helping the poor might actually increase their reliance on handouts and complicate the search for a long-term solution. We are attracted to slogans like "God helps those who help themselves," which we have elevated to almost-scriptural status. (That saying, by the way, is from Aesop's fables, and goes "The gods help them that help themselves.") We worry that the poor may be undeserving and so our handouts won't really help. We see poor people in the grocery store purchasing frivolous junk food and decide they aren't entitled to our help. We conclude that the poor are poor because they are lazy, ignorant, or stupid. Is that really our attitude? Do we really believe that grace should be given only to those who deserve it? If we think this way, we are ungodly. For God helps those who *don't* help themselves. Indeed, the essence of grace is giving to the undeserving. God gives to us in spite of the fact that we are unworthy. We should do the same for others. It is simply what Christians do.

shutting off compassion

Concluding that the poor are undeserving causes us to shut up our "bowels of compassion" (1 John 3:17 KJV), which in turn shuts down our inclination toward lovingkindness. It is a kind of charity constipation. As our clenched-fist attitude toward the poor spreads, we gradually become a stingy person. Eventually, we withhold generosity from even our loved ones because they, too, are undeserving. Charity is the antidote to this tight-fisted, stingy, lonely life. In the discipline of charity, we happily give to the poor whether they are deserving or not. After all, the Bible does not call us to help only the deserving needy. It simply commands us to give alms to the poor. In this we are called to be like God. He did not stoop to save us because we deserved it. He rescued us because he loved us. Our salvation by God is the ultimate act of charity awarded to totally undeserving spiritual paupers. So when we help the poor—*especially* the undeserving ones—we are being like God. And we will gain as much from our act of charity as the poor do.

the role of government

Governments do more for the poor today than they did in Bible times. But even the ancient Israelites were required to give a "poor tithe" for the social programs of the day. They were also commanded to personally give alms, above this poor tithe. Admittedly, the situation is more complicated today. Some of our taxes do go to help the poor. That should be good news to us; we have a head start on almsgiving. But we need to finish the work we have begun. Perhaps we need to start thinking of a portion of our taxes as alms and cheerfully pay them. That might improve our attitude when taxes are due. However, few of us would say, "The government should do it all!" We recognize the need for charity above and beyond government programs, and individuals seem to do charity better than governments or groups do anyway. Few of us get the same satisfaction from paying taxes that we get from helping a person we know by name. Governments can provide a basic safety net for the poor, but we Christians can step in and provide the rest, along with meeting even deeper spiritual needs that no government can meet.

defining poverty

How bad off do people have to be for us to consider them poor? Most of us are tempted to draw the poverty line so low that we'll seldom or never meet anyone whom we could really label *poor*. We see needy people around us and say, "There are millions of people around the world who would love to exchange places with them," thereby excusing ourselves from helping them. So who should we help? The answer to that question is another question: Who did Jesus help? He helped those in need. He did not ask if they were frugal, deserved a handout, were reckless, or had sinned and caused their own sickness. He helped them because he had the resources they needed. He even helped the rich when he could. He did not say, "This military commander is far better off than I; why should I heal his son?" (see Matt. 8:5–13). He simply helped whoever he could because he is very God and that is what God does. We should too.

the poor and evangelism

It is no coincidence that virtually every great evangelistic revival in history has been accompanied by a parallel revival in caring for the poor. A burden for lost souls and concern for the poor are twin passions; they feed on each other. Could it be that the lack of passion for souls that is so common in today's church is related to our lack of concern for the poor? If we were better at helping those with empty hearts, would we get better at helping those with empty shelves? Or vice versa? After all, both evangelism and charity spring from the same source: loving compassion.

actively seeking the needy

How could we refuse a hungry person if we knew they were really hungry? No Christian would. Even people who aren't Christians help poor people when confronted with a need. Christians do not fail when they see needs up close; we just fail by arranging our lives so that we never see needy people. If we saw them, we would help them. Most of us can go weeks or months without seeing a poor person. We circulate in different orbits than they do. But Christians should find the needy. Just as we are commanded to find those in spiritual poverty and bring them riches in Christ, we are likewise commanded to find those in material poverty and bring them aid. Most people help those in need when they happen to see them. Christians should search out needy people. We are evangelistic about both bodies and souls. We need to go to the highways and byways, searching for needy people as described in the story of the great banquet in Luke 14. We don't just hang about our cozy homes and comfortable churches promising we'll help the poor if they show up; most of them never will. Serious Christians get into lifeboats and go to sea to rescue people in need, refusing to sit in our warm lighthouses waiting for the shipwrecked to wash up on shore. Christ came to seek and save the lost. We Christians should do the same.

giving our time

It may be harder to give our time than our money. For some of us, money is more plentiful than time. Charitable organizations are desperate for volunteers. When we volunteer our time, more aid gets to the poor because the organization does not have to hire people to do the work. Another advantage of giving time over money is that it increases the change in our hearts. Who finds the same satisfaction in writing a check as in serving a meal to a needy person? The Good Samaritan probably found greater joy in helping the beaten traveler face-to-face than he had found in paying that year's poor tithe. Those of us who call ourselves Christians might consider giving our time along with our money. We'd be happier people if we did. That is not to say that the poor are always grateful. Sometimes they're abusive and do not express the sort of thanks we think they should. But we don't either when it comes to God's grace given to us. Perhaps for that reason alone we ought to help the ungrateful poor, because it's like looking in a mirror.

the invisible poor

The trouble with the notion that charity begins at home (popularized by Charles Dickens) is that most of us don't get far enough away from home to see the needy people who don't happen to live nearby. But God loves them too. While beginning our charity at home seems like a nice notion, charity shouldn't begin and end at home. Our commission is global, not just local. The greatest poverty in our world is found across oceans in out-of-the way places we will most likely never visit. The plight of the world's poor breaks God's heart, and he expects us to do something about it. It's been said that six million children die of hunger every year. Certainly, these souls deserve our attention, don't they? The Bible says that God "so loved *the world*" (John 3:16, emphasis added). While we quibble about welfare benefits for the poor in our own nations, millions more starve to death far from our homes. They do not want a shirt or pair of pants; they want something to eat or water to drink so they can survive one more day. At times entire countries become death camps due to famine. They are full of gaunt, emaciated, ghostlike people who lack enough food and water to reach tomorrow. These needy people lie broken and bleeding by the global roadside, too weak to call for our help. They are largely out of our sight. What should we do? What would Jesus do? What did the Good Samaritan do? The answer is obvious. We Christians will send whatever aid we can. It is the Christlike thing to do. What else could we do? Go golfing to forget these people?

spiritual gains

Charity is good work, but what makes it a *spiritual* discipline? The answer is simple: Taking up the discipline of charity brings us closer to God. As we do his work, we find ourselves beside him. God is already with the poor. And when we show up, we find him near. We will face him one day, and he will remind us of the treatment we gave him. *Him?* Yes, when we help the needy, we are judged by Christ to have fed, clothed, visited, and cared for Christ himself (Matt. 25). And the poor themselves will sometimes inspire our faith. We will develop new levels of gratitude and sense God's blessing on our labor. We will often see among the poor greater generosity than we see among our friends. Even if we cure nothing at all and fail to change the world one bit, *we* will be changed because charity is a means of grace. As we make the world a better place, God makes us better people. It is in giving that we receive.

how to begin practicing charity

celebrate what you are already doing

Assess what you are already doing. Many Christians are more involved with the poor than they realize. Take an honest assessment of what you are doing personally and what your family and church are doing to help the poor. Find out what percentage of your taxes goes to poor people, and celebrate it. Don't let this chapter make you feel like a bad Christian. Instead, let it inspire you to become a better one. Start by celebrating what you are already doing.

plan a drive-through

If you feel distant from the poor in your community, plan a Sunday afternoon drive, not in the country, but through the area of your town where needy people live. Drive slowly and let God lay a burden on your heart. If you can, stop and visit people, not to help yet, but to learn, feel, and make friends.

begin even if you don't feel compassion

Even if you feel no compassion for the poor, start doing something to help them. After all, that's why we call it a spiritual *discipline*; it takes determination. You can help the poor without feeling compassion, but you cannot do it for long. Seeing poverty face-to-face has a way of bringing out Christ's compassion that is deep in our hearts.

start a food pantry

A food pantry won't solve the world's hunger problem, but it is a start. Face it—nothing you do will solve the world's poverty problem, nor will anything you do solve the world's sin problem. But we should each do what we can anyway. It is in trying that we obey God's commands. So start with a simple act like organizing a food pantry at your church or even for your Sunday school class or small group.

start volunteering your time this week

If you were to become an active volunteer serving poor people, to what organization would you contribute your time? What is your favorite charitable organization? Why not start this week by taking the first step: calling to offer your time.

sign up for a mission trip

Sign up for a trip where you will see abject poverty that will haunt you for the rest of your life. See poverty as God sees it, up close and personal. You will be permanently altered if you do this, so will everyone you live with. It may be better to spend your money on this trip than to give it to your poor nephew struggling to pay his college tuition. When you have seen the world as God sees it, you will be forever changed.

take an offering for the poor

In some churches, any non-designated offering received on the first Sunday of each month goes to almsgiving. When might your church take an offering to help the poor, as Christ expects us to do? Or when could your small group do it? Or if nobody else seems excited at the prospect, when could you take an offering from yourself and see that it helps the poor?

adopt a new lifestyle

This book only asks you to try a spiritual discipline for one week then move on to another. Yet some of these disciplines would make good lifelong habits. Most Christians will practice prayer or Bible reading the rest of their lives. Few will do that with this discipline. Is God calling you to take up this discipline in a more serious way, representing the rest who will pass it by and forget it by next month?

what about you?

What are your specific plans to practice the discipline of charity this week?

12. prayer

In the same way, the Spirit helps us in our weakness. We do not know what we ought to pray for, but the Spirit himself intercedes for us with groans that words cannot express.

—Romans 8:26

Prayer is a conversation with God through which we come to know him better and develop greater reliance on him. Prayer is less about asking and getting things from God than about getting things right. Prayer is a means of drawing near to God and sensing him draw near to us. In prayer, we pledge allegiance to God and assert our total reliance on his grace. It is perhaps the oldest and most fundamental spiritual discipline, preceding Scripture by several thousand years.

an intangible discipline

While we know prayer is important, most of us in the Western world don't practice prayer very well. We're too task oriented. We want to get something done, check something off our to-do lists, and make some progress. Maybe this is why we prefer Bible reading to prayer. We can count the chapters we've read or verses we've memorized and see measurable progress. Prayer, however, is so . . . *spiritual*. And we are more a practical people than a spiritual people.

reasons to pray

Prayer is much more than asking God for things. In prayer, we also praise God for his goodness, confess our sins, express gratitude, confirm our faith, and draw closer to God. At its core, prayer is about cultivating a relationship with God. It is about communion, fellowship, and even union with God. Prayer binds us to God so that we gain his perspective. It does not change his mind so much as it changes *our* minds and hearts. After being with God, we see the glaring disparity between his values and the world's ideals, the church's values and even our own standards. We begin to feel God's emotions, think God's thoughts, and want God's will. Prayer is not just about changing life; it's about changing *us*. In short, prayer is a means of sanctifying us, of spiritually forming us into an image of God's own Son.

Prayer is also a powerful personal statement of faith. It is hard to pray without believing in God. By praying we proclaim that we indeed believe in God. Prayer is our personal statement of faith, our pledge of allegiance to God. An anemic prayer life illustrates a feeble faith. How can we assert there is a God if we don't talk to him? Prayer is the voice of faith.

how to pray

So how should we pray? Jesus' disciples asked the same question. We don't know exactly what they thought of Jesus' answer. We do know that most evangelicals don't think much of it. Jesus replied to the disciples' question by giving them a prayer to say; we call it the Lord's Prayer. Most of us don't like to repeat a fixed prayer. We like variety and think we can pray in our own words better than using the words Jesus taught us to pray. So we pretend that Scripture means, "Pray after this pattern." We would not fit in with the early Christians who took Christ's words to mean exactly what they say. Those Christians prayed the Lord's Prayer itself. In fact, they prayed it three times a day every single day. But most evangelicals in fleeing formal religion have abandoned praying the prayer Christ taught and thus do not take his teaching literally, on this point anyway. Perhaps we are right; maybe the Lord's Prayer was intended only as a model, and the early Christians got it wrong. But before we discard the prayer itself, we should remember that the early church prayed this prayer daily in worship and that the vast majority of Christians have prayed this exact prayer for two thousand years. So perhaps we might pray it at least occasionally. Some Christians pray the Lord's Prayer before each meal. It is an error to take the Lord's Prayer lightly. Some do that by praying it too much with such ritual blandness that they forget its meaning. Others take it lightly by praying it too little with such abandonment of ritual that they also forget its meaning. Mainline Christians may make the first error, but evangelicals are certainly guilty of the second.

what to pray about

If we did determine that the Lord's Prayer is an outline for praying, what does it teach us about prayer? The prayer begins by teaching us the relationship we have in prayer is that of a child to a loving *Father*. The prayer then immediately redirects our minds from earthly things to God's abode, *heaven*. We are taught adoration as we *hallow* God's name. This initial focus on God and heaven aligns our values with God's so that when we return to earthly matters, we pray about God's concerns first, God's *kingdom* coming on earth so that his *will is done* here *on earth* the way it is *in heaven*. Then we pray for personal needs. We ask for *daily bread*, the essentials needed to sustain life, but then quickly shift to asking *forgiveness* of our sins, saying that we have forgiven others. Speaking of sin, we are taught to plead for escape from *temptation* and deliverance *from evil*. Then Protestants close with a final doxology of praise that was added sometime after Jesus taught the prayer, acknowledging that to God belongs the *kingdom, power, and glory forever*.

What a glimpse into God's prayer list! Perhaps we improve on Christ's original words in our casual, ad-lib prayers, but we will not improve on his content. Christ taught us to praise God, pray about his kingdom, our necessities, forgiveness, temptation, and deliverance from evil. Even if we use the Lord's Prayer as a model prayer and not an actual prayer to be prayed, most Christians will have to adjust their prayer outline to the things Jesus taught us to pray about. This will mean more prayer for the kingdom of God and spiritual matters like temptation and sin and less prayer about our own requests and the guidance we want to receive from God. Throughout history, those who have thought they could improve on the original instructions of Christ have faded away. But the Lord's Prayer always makes a comeback.

In order to resist the temptation to make self-centered prayers, Christians often use the Lord's Prayer as an outline. By sticking to its agenda, they monitor the balance of their prayers. Others use the familiar ACTS acronym (Adoration, Confession, Thanksgiving, and Supplication) to do the same. By whatever means, most of us need to find a way to become less self-centered and more kingdom-centered in our praying.

adoration

Great prayer warriors almost always begin their prayers with adoration, giving God glory and praise for who he is. Adoration is not thanking God; it is adoring him for his essence and character. It is not that God has poor self-esteem and needs to be cheered up; God does not need our sweet talk. We need to confess God's greatness so we are reminded of it ourselves. By doing homework on the traits of God, we can learn what it is about him that we should adore, and we can upgrade this part of our praying to include adoration. Bible study (especially of Psalms) helps us know the character of God so that we won't skip over adoration or substitute thanksgiving, mislabeling it as praise. Adoration makes known the character of God.

confession

In confession, we admit our sins to God and ourselves. Confession is coming clean before God. If we confess our sins, he is faithful and will forgive us. Unconfessed sin is a barrier to relationship with God, blocking us from drawing near. When we bring it all out into the light, we clear away that obstruction. Being honest with God ends our pretence that there is nothing wrong between God and us. Confession is admitting to God that we are who we are and that without him, we'd be even worse. Refusing to tell God our hidden thoughts, feelings, attitudes, and desires keeps no secrets from God. Pretending to hide our true selves from God only perpetuates a false notion in our own minds. And no relationship can move far when one party is not honest. But there are things to confess besides sin. We confess our weaknesses and tendencies so that these, too, are brought into the light. We even confess our temptations. We acknowledge our own frailty and total dependence on God. When we confess, we see ourselves as we really are and become more dependent on God's grace. True and open confession introduces us to ourselves; we see ourselves as God sees us.

thanksgiving

In thanksgiving, we recite God's mighty acts, expressing gratitude for what he has done throughout history and in our own lives. We do not do this because God forgets what he has done and needs reminding; we do it because *we* forget. We thank God for calling Abraham, for bringing the children of Israel through the Red Sea, for establishing the nation of Israel, and for raising up King David. We thank God for calling the prophets and blessing and punishing the various kings. We thank him for sending his Son, Jesus, and we thank him for what Jesus did to heal the sick, raise the dead, and preach liberty. We thank God for raising Jesus from the dead, for establishing the church, for inspiring Christians to write the books of the New Testament, and for leading the church to select the right books for our Bible over the course of several hundred years. We thank God for his work around the world today and for all who serve him. We thank God for how he is working in other churches and denominations. Finally, after thanking God for several thousand years' worth of graciousness, we are ready to turn to the present and our own lives. We thank him for our own parents and families and for his provision and providence for our loved ones and ourselves. We recite in detail his mighty acts done specifically for us. We thank him for good and bad things because they both help us become more like Christ. Only after such a recitation of thanksgiving are we ready to ask God for anything.

supplication

Supplication is asking God for something. This sort of praying is also called petition or sometimes intercession when asking God on behalf of others. We are totally helpless and utterly reliant on him so we make our requests known to him. We even ask for things we think we'd get without asking, training ourselves to be thankful when any good thing comes our way. In supplication, we make our desires known to God. Sometimes we desire things that really aren't good for us, and God purifies our desires during prayer so that while we first asked amiss, we later ask rightly. God does indeed answer prayer. God can be moved by his children's prayers; thus, we have a part in the outcome of things. We can affect the outcome of events through prayer. So we boldly go before God's throne, asking our Father the King to grant our requests. We are bold but not presumptuous because we know that Jesus Christ, the model pray-er, ended his own desperate prayer in the garden of Gethsemane with the words, "Not my will, but yours be done" (Luke 22:42).

listening

Prayer is a conversation. A good conversation shouldn't be one sided. Prayer ought to be two-way and not a one-sided monologue. God is a good listener, but he also has some things to say. It is poor manners to do all the talking. Prayer is a dialogue, not a filibuster. People who are good at prayer often shut up and listen. Some of us like talking too much. We like hearing ourselves talk, and our prayers are not about God and his concerns, but about us and our concerns. For us, prayer is a chance to talk to ourselves while God sits in the audience. Talkative people might need to discipline themselves to start listening for God's side of the conversation in prayer. He will speak if we let him get a word in edgewise.

how to begin practicing prayer

start a daily prayer time

Pick a time each day this week for daily prayer. Stick to the schedule for an entire week.

set a time for extended prayer

Pick at least one longer time period this week in which you will do nothing but pray. Don't check anything off your list, and don't measure your progress by reading or writing. Practice the pure *spiritual* discipline of prayer.

pray the Scriptures

If you feel tongue-tied when you pray, simply look up the great prayers of the Bible and pray them. They were good enough to be written down for us, so why not use them? Simply turn to Psalms or the Epistles and seek out the prayers that best fit your needs, then pray them fervently.

make a prayer outline

Are your prayers balanced? A prayer outline helps us police our prayers to make sure we give appropriate weight to items we might rush past to get to our favorite, more self-centered parts. What would you include in your own prayer outline? What are the categories you ought to cover in prayer? In what order? Turn your answers into an outline you can follow in prayer.

journal your prayers

Written prayers do not have to be stale and repetitive. They can be more meaningful, more thoughtful, and more powerful in their effect on you. If you enjoy writing, carefully write down your prayers, then use them to pray fervently.

start a prayer list

What are you praying for specifically? Do you keep a record of answers you receive to prayers? Make a list of the requests you want to regularly bring to God. However, when making the list, integrate it to a full outline so you won't be trapped into thinking prayer is mostly supplication. Include the other elements of balanced prayer on your prayer list as well.

daily pray the Lord's Prayer

Just in case the early Christians were right about this habit, try it for a week. Where could you fit the Lord's Prayer into your life three times each day, usually tied to another habitual act? When you wake up? When you go to sleep? When you eat meals? When you're driving? Think of three occasions during the course of a day when you could pray this prayer deliberately and carefully.

pray in the middle of the night

Do you ever wake at night and find that you can't get back to sleep for awhile? Pray during these periods—every time. Instead of counting sheep, talk to the Shepherd.

plan a prayer retreat

If you are taking the discipline of prayer seriously, how about making plans for a prayer retreat, during which you would devote an entire day—perhaps even several days—entirely to prayer? Picking the date is the first step to making this happen.

what about you?

What are your specific plans to practice the discipline of prayer this week?

13. penance

The Lord disciplines those he loves, and he punishes everyone he accepts as a son. Endure hardship as discipline; God is treating you as sons. For what son is not disciplined by his father? If you are not disciplined (and everyone undergoes discipline), then you are illegitimate children and not true sons.

—Hebrews 12:6–8

Penance is willfully embracing earthly punishment for wrongdoing that has already been forgiven by God. It is done to rectify past wrongs and to make us better people. Penance brings us into reconciliation with others and ourselves. Penance is the spiritual discipline of "doing our time" for what we have done wrong and making things right. In this discipline, we do not try to earn God's forgiveness, but assign consequences to ourselves for our wrongdoings. When we wrong others, penance voluntarily makes it up to them by balancing the earthly books. Penance is a means of disciplining and training ourselves.

the reason for penance

Most Protestants shun the notion of penance. We think it's too Catholic or that it's a way of earning God's forgiveness. Protestants believe there is nothing we can do to earn favor from God. Thus, penance implies salvation by works to us. But that is a grave misunderstanding of this discipline. Penance is for Protestants and Catholics alike; it is a *Christian* discipline. God's grace is indeed free of charge and comes through faith, not by human effort. But penance is not about bettering our relationship with God or earning forgiveness of sins. It is primarily about our relationship with others and ourselves. It is we who need to shed the burden of past wrongs that we still carry, burdens God has already forgiven! The spiritual discipline of penance often helps free us of these self-imposed burdens of guilt. And it trains us to avoid committing the same wrongs in the future.

forgiveness and consequences

If God doesn't need our penance, then who does? Others do, and we do. Being forgiven by God does not automatically make things right with the people we've wronged. Consider the case of a pastor who is caught in a motel room with one of his parishioners. How quickly can God forgive this pastor? In a second. At the moment of true repentance, the pastor's slate will be cleared and the debt totally forgiven by God. But while God can forgive in an instant, humans naturally take longer. The church people whom this pastor deceived, along with his wife, will take longer to be reconciled to him than God will. Most church members think such a pastor should stop preaching. They would say he shouldn't act as if nothing happened or keep pastoring that church. Consider the case of a criminal found guilty of murder who becomes a Christian while serving a life sentence in prison. Should this person go free because he or she has been fully forgiven by God? Many Christians would say the murderer should still do the time or pay his or her debt to society even though the slate has been cleared with God.

Most of us assume that people still have to face the temporal consequences for their wrongdoings even though they have escaped the eternal penalty. If we think this way, we have understood the core idea of the spiritual discipline of penance. It is taking on earthly punishment for wrongdoing as a means of grace, a channel through which God makes us better people and brings us into reconciliation with others. In penance, we willingly take on punishment as a means of making things right and training ourselves for the future. Penance is the discipline of paying our debts to others even though our debts to God has been paid in full.

Penance and restitution are so similar that they are hard to differentiate. Indeed, if we don't like the term *penance*, we might substitute *restitution* and arrive at the same place. However, restitution generally requires another party with whom to be reconciled, while penance is sometimes general in nature and related more to ourselves than to the people we have offended. Also, penance can relate to groups we have wronged. Zacchaeus may have practiced both kinds of penance. He promised direct restitution to individuals he swindled, and he also promised to commit half of his wealth to the poor (see Luke 19). The first act is what we often call restitution; the second is penance.

"little" sins

Most of us would agree that there should be penance for things like murder. In fact, the term *penitentiary*, now merely a synonym for *prison*, has its root in the idea of penance. And most of us agree that a mere "I'm sorry" responded to with "No problem" is not an adequate way of dealing with the adulterous pastor mentioned above. We can understand the need for penance after such "big" sins as these. But we balk at doing penance for wrongs we ourselves are guilty of—what we have labeled "little" sins. Yet it is our personal, seemingly minor offenses that penance is precisely designed to remedy.

Penance is a means of grace. Used rightly, it is a channel through which God changes us, helps us grow, and enables us to overcome sin and our wayward temperaments. It helps us stop doing wrong. It forms us into the image of Christ. When we take on the discipline of penance, we assign ourselves penalties for our wrongs in order to improve our behaviors. These penalties do not earn forgiveness from God any more than our children's punishment earns our forgiveness. Penance is our training for the future. We use penance when we've spent an hour in a committee meeting and leave realizing we made several harsh and cutting remarks to one particular person. Penance is for people who recall how badly they treated a girl back in high school but realize it would not be wise to contact her now. Penance is for the dad who promised his daughter to attend every single soccer game this year but just missed her second game. Penance is for the wife who realizes she has been ill-tempered all evening. Penance is for the employer who now admits he paid his workers less than they deserved for many years. Penance is for the person who used to toss trash out the car window when driving at night. It is for the middle-aged woman who remembers how cruelly she treated her now-deceased mother years ago. In short, penance is for everyone except perfect people. It is for all sins, even "little" sins, past and present wrongs, offenses committed by us personally and as a group.

family discipline

Parents intuitively understand penance. In an act of rage, a young boy destroys his sister's science project the night before it is due. What do the parents do? They try to get the brother to repent. They demand he apologize to his sister. But is that all? Not for most parents. There will be consequences for his wrong-doing. Thus, children are sometimes spanked, sent to their rooms, grounded, or socially excluded by getting a time-out to ponder misdeeds. Do these punishments mean the parent has not forgiven the child? Not at all! Parents simply don't want to let their children off the hook with a quick apology. They fear the children might assume they can do anything they please if they merely say "I'm sorry" afterward. So most parents take some action to discipline their children, to teach and train them, steering them away from anarchy and toward civilization. Penance brings this training to grown-ups too.

three steps after wrongdoing

The first thing to do when we sin is to ask for forgiveness from God. This is the easier part, which is why it is the only part done by many Christians. Figuring God's forgiveness is all we need, we merrily go on our way, presuming the slate is clear. But it's not, at least not completely.

Our wrong actions hurt others too. So the second step is going to the people we've wronged and asking for their forgiveness. This is much harder than asking God for forgiveness. We all hate to say, "I was wrong," but we must in order to bring reconciliation. How blessed are those who take the second step to gain forgiveness from people they've wronged!

But there is also a third step: penance. Most Christians understand the idea of penance when applied to stealing, for example. "Simply pay it back," we say. Or perhaps we'd say, "Pay it back with interest." Indeed, Jesus considered Zacchaeus's penance as clear evidence that he had indeed been changed. But the hard kind of penance is not financial, but relational, righting the books with the people we've wronged. We might be willing to ask forgiveness, but should we then walk away free and clear? Human life does not work that way. If you've been secretly working for several years at destroying a coworker's reputation, asking for his or her forgiveness is not enough. There is damage to repair. If you took up the discipline of penance, you'd set about an intentional campaign to reverse the effects of your years of undermining your coworker. That could take years as opposed to tossing a mere "I'm sorry" to the violated person. Receiving forgiveness from God is easy and quick; receiving it from others is tricky and slow. Doing penance is the hardest and slowest of all. That is why this discipline is so rarely practiced. But penance is powerful in making us more like Christ. It is hard but completely worth it.

penance as training

Penance is training. It provides the discipline to break bad habits and start good ones. Breaking a habit sometimes takes a bit of pain. In one company, the executives all wore rubber bands on their wrists, and they agreed to snap the bands hard any time they said the words *impossible* or *can't*. What began as a lighthearted stunt completely changed the atmosphere of the company. Self-imposed penance is like snapping that rubber band. It is snapping ourselves for our wrongs in order to train ourselves to do right.

quiet penance

Penance is best done in secret. We have done wrong, and we know it. We feel compelled to balance the books and pay our debts, so we take on this discipline. But we ought to do it quietly. Indeed, penance does not always have to be related to the offended people or offense itself in order to be successful. We could decide that for the rest of our lives we'll pick up trash every time we walk for exercise, not as a good deed but as an act of penance. We could determine to always return the shopping cart plus one other every time we go grocery shopping to remind us of the past wrongs we've done and to humble us. Or our acts of penance might be directly related to our offenses. If we seldom visited an aged parent in his or her final years, we might determine to go to a nursing home on the first Sunday of each month to visit people we don't know. Would we benefit from this ministry? Certainly we would. But reminding ourselves each month of our unkindness in the past might train us to be more kind in the present and future. These are the sorts of things we do as the spiritual discipline of penance.

inner peace

Penance brings inner peace. God forgives us in a moment, and others may come to forgive us in time. But the hardest forgiveness to gain is often from ourselves. We may be forgiven for that deed we did long ago, yet still feel guilty. Even after the person we wronged hugs us and tells us all is forgotten, we continue to feel guilty. Why? Often it is because we have not forgiven ourselves.

The wealthy oil magnate who swindled his rancher brother out of the family ranch still feels guilty, even though he went forward at the Billy Graham rally in Dallas. What's wrong? His brother is dead and gone, but the rich man still feels guilty. The accusing finger he senses is his own. This man should take up the discipline of penance. The more the oilman makes things right, the less he will feel guilty. God forgave him freely and without cost. But the oilman also knows in his heart that to keep the books right on earth somehow requires paying his debt to society. He can do it with money or through serving others. What will make his actions a means of grace is his willingness to take on the discipline while believing that it is just that—a means God is using to make him a better person. He will come to know joy and freedom after doing penance. He will feel free again as he did when he was a boy on the ranch. He will be released from the death grip of his self-inflicted guilt. In the discipline of penance, he will come to find the hardest forgiveness of all: forgiveness of himself.

the danger of penance

We must close this chapter as we began it: by reminding ourselves that this discipline can be a dangerous one. When we take on this spiritual discipline, it will be easy to let our minds slip into thinking that penance is something between God and us. If we do, it will become one more baby step on the path toward imagining that God is impressed with our good deeds and is piling them on the scales to outweigh the bad things we've done, finally tipping the balance toward heaven. This is false. Penance is not about God and us. It is about our relationships with others and with ourselves. In penance, we pay off our horizontal debt (to others), not our vertical debt (to God). We also find inner peace and personal satisfaction as we come to feel fully forgiven by others and ourselves.

how to begin practicing penance

ponder past wrongs

Begin by setting aside some time for pondering the deeds for which you would do penance. What are some things you've done that have been forgiven by God but are still out of balance with others? Don't become depressed by listing dozens of past wrongs. All you need is one or two to begin this discipline. Try to ignore the wrongs done by others and stick with your own. Avoid thinking, "Well, they were wrong in that situation too." Worry more about the plank in your own eye than the speck in another's.

gain forgiveness first

This chapter is not directly about forgiveness and reconciliation but penance. However, if you need forgiveness, get that first before doing penance. If all this is too complicated to undertake this week, select another area to work on now and put the forgive-ness matter on hold. But make an appointment to meet soon with your pastor to discuss what steps you need to take in seeking forgiveness.

pick a penance action

What act could you do to balance the books between you and the person or entity you wronged? Will you do a related action or an unrelated one?

start this week

Take your first action of penance this week. How will you know what it is like if you don't at least try it?

think about group sins

Have you been part of an entity that sinned as a group? If so, begin contemplating what might be done to deal with this matter. Do not rush too quickly to action, simply begin pondering this week, and perhaps chat only with one other person about it.

what about you?

What are your specific plans to practice the discipline of penance this week?

PART 3
disciplines of relationships

In the disciplines of relationships, we practice the actions that make right our relationships with others. When the term *spiritual disciplines* is used, most of us think of praying, fasting, or having devotions, but God is more concerned about our personal relationships than our personal devotions. That is why Christ gave the radical advice to even leave worship to go make things right with others. These disciplines involve outwardly making things right between us and others by making restitution or restoring fallen Christians, but they also involve inwardly making things right with others by taking captive our own thoughts about others or purifying our ambitions so that we are not stomping on everyone else. These are the lesser-known spiritual disciplines, but they are actually just as important because our relationships with others are but a reflection of our relationships with God.

A wrong relationship with others indicates a wrong relationship with God. But cultivating and maintaining right relationships takes discipline—spiritual discipline.

giving back & making things right. restore what was damaged.

MT 5:23:24

14. restitution

I strive always to keep my conscience clear before God and man.

—*Acts 24:16*

When I was in seventh grade, my church youth group had a Halloween party, and I didn't have a costume. My friend John and I stopped at the local J. J. Newberry's store on the way home from school to shop. Among the array of Halloween masks and costumes was a first-rate stick-on mustache packaged in a little plastic case. I could imagine myself wearing this mustache for the party, causing all the girls to swoon. So, I tried it on. Somehow it made me feel taller, more manly, and mature. The problem, however, was that I had no money.

I don't think I'd ever stolen anything before that. I slipped that little mustache in the right pocket of my school jacket and sneaked out to the street. I wore it to the party. The girls didn't swoon.

I had a hard time forgetting that mustache. I knew I was wrong to steal it, and that I should go back to the store, confess, and pay for it. But I was afraid. I feared both the embarrassment and the penalty. A lady who worked at Newberry's attended the church where my dad pastored. I figured she'd tell him, and my dad would punish me like the thief I was. I conjured all kinds of worst-case scenario endings. I kept remembering the large flier posted near the entrance to that store. It had a drawing of a teenager peering through the bars in a jail cell. Above his sad face it read, "Shoplifters go to jail."

I could visualize a whole newspaper spread on how nice teens—even a preacher's son—could go bad. *I* would be the illustration. Parents would whisper after church, "Doesn't it make your heart ache, you know, how the Drury boy turned out?" They would admonish each other, "Keep a tight rein on your kids, or they'll turn out like the *preacher's* kid."

So I never went back. Each time I recalled my offense, I'd try to ignore it, excuse it, or dismiss it. At first I told myself I couldn't afford making things right. I simply didn't have the money. The mustache had already lost its stickiness, so returning it wouldn't suffice. I didn't want to get my friend John in trouble either. I figured they'd make him out to be an accessory or something. Mostly, I just put it off. I intended to make it right . . . eventually.

With time, my conviction gradually disappeared, and I almost forgot about it. Occasionally, guilt would surface, but I would dismiss it with comments like, "It was such a little thing," or, "Oh my, that was a long time ago." I graduated from high school and moved away to college, forgetting the little mustache. For the most part, that is. But every time I'd hear about restitution,

I'd remember the mustache. When I'd read about restitution in an article or hear someone share a testimony about restitution they had made, that mustache would come slithering back to haunt me. The mustache was always there, reminding me of an unmade restitution.

At a retreat two decades later, God convinced me of the necessity of this restitution. It was clear I'd better fix it soon. I knew that if I delayed much longer, it would be more than foot dragging; it would be outright disobedience, even rebellion.

Within a month, I was in the area with my family. I loaded my five-year-old son David into the car and went to make restitution for what I had stolen twenty years before. I explained to my son what I had done and what I was about to do. Frankly, all the way to the store I was secretly hoping it had gone out of business. It hadn't. David was intrigued by this whole idea. He seemed to get a kick out of seeing his dad humbled.

After paying for the mustache, we returned to the car and headed out of town. My son had said nothing throughout the whole process, but I could sense his mind whirling. As we drove up the entry ramp of the interstate, he turned and said, "You know, Dad, it would be better if you'd never take things. Then you wouldn't have to go back like that."

I think he got the point. I know I got *David's* point!

Restitution is going back and making things right for things you took or with people you hurt. It is restoring to the original owners what is rightfully theirs—be it property, respect, or reputation. Restitution is returning a tool box taken from the company years ago. It is paying for the stack of office supplies you slipped out of the office without anyone's knowledge. It is paying taxes on unreported income you hid from the tax man. Restitution is large utility companies granting refunds because they illegally overcharged their customers. It is an airline giving rebates to travelers because they have been guilty of unfair competition.

But restitution deals with more than property. It is also going back and making things right for hurtful things said or done. It's far easier for me to reveal my mustache story than to tell you of the difficult and painful times I've had to ask my wife, sons, bosses, friends, and assistants to forgive me. Restitution is asking forgiveness for harsh words, a quick tongue, or cutting remarks. It is asking forgiveness from a brother we hurt, a mother we caused heartache, or a former spouse we maligned. Restitution is confessing and seeking forgiveness from an old business partner, neighbor, or roommate. It is admitting our past errors in relationships and humbly seeking forgiveness from the ones we have hurt. And it's harder to make personal restitution than property restitution.

Restitution is a discipline in humility. Pride and restitution are incompatible. It's not popular or easy. And it is one of the most painful disciplines of the obedient life. But it is biblical. It is the Christian way. Any who seriously seek to follow the teachings of Jesus Christ will walk the painful restitution path at times. Serious followers of the Master will hunger for an easily convicted, tender heart. We will thirst for a soft, easily pricked conscience. And we will act on these promptings, returning to the offended party to make things right. It is the Christian way.

why make restitution?

What would possess a Christian to take such humiliating steps? Why have believers throughout history practiced this discipline? Are there any good reasons to put ourselves through such a torturous experience? Yes. Here are seven good reasons to make restitution.

restitution is a matter of obedience

More than fifteen times, the Old Testament teaches restitution for followers of God. Jesus confirmed the idea in the New Testament, even recognizing restitution as one of the evidences that "salvation has come to this house" (Luke 19:9). Not that making restitution can save a person. Nothing we can do will bring salvation, except trusting Christ. But the Bible expects restitution to be the kind of thing we do if we follow God. It's consistent with all other teaching in Scripture. The reason we don't like it is not because it's unbiblical, but because restitution is in total opposition to our pride. We hate to be humbled, embarrassed, or humiliated. It goes against human nature, so we would rather save our pride than make restitution. But the Word stands unrevised by our tardiness in obedience. The single best reason to make restitution is because God said to do it. It is a matter of obedience (John 14:15).

restitution reinforces personal happiness

Obedience brings happiness, not a silly, frivolous kind of giddiness, but a deep-seated joy of knowing that we are living up to what we have been commanded to do. We may have asked God to forgive us of theft or an interpersonal justice, and he has fully washed it away. Then why do we still feel guilty? It is horizontal guilt and not vertical guilt from God. We continue to sense a sort of unresolved blame from others.

When we leave a restitution unmade, we add a load of guilt to the burdens of our daily walk. We feel guilty. Once we've made wrongs right, that load of horizontal guilt is lifted. We try to shoo our unmade restitutions into the dark recesses of our minds, but they will periodically fly up like bats from a cave. Once restitution is made, we experience a new happiness and freedom in our lives. Then we wonder why we took so long to do it. We are happier (and holier) people after we make restitution.

restitution releases us to greater service

Unmade restitutions are like giant monkeys on our backs. Satan slides up to our ears every time we try to do something for God. He whispers, "Where do you think you're going? We both know what kind of person you are. Remember how you . . . ?" When restitutions are all made, there is a new boldness to serve Christ in other areas.

restitution removes another's stumbling block

Do we ever think other people may hold grudges against us for what we said or did long ago? Have we ever thought the offended people may be sour, bitter, and resentful over the "little thing" we did? To be sure, they are sinning. But aren't we accessories to their sin? Are we providing opportunities for them to continue in sin? What would happen if we approached them to humbly ask for their forgiveness? What if they granted forgiveness to us? Could they hold a grudge any longer? Our tardiness in making restitution may be placing a great stumbling block in others' paths toward God.

restitution releases us to teach others

If we needed to advise other believers on the advantages of restitution, what stories would we tell? My dad once told me an unforgettable story of how among his tools he found a hatchet owned by the church district where he had served years before. He told me how he rationalized it at first, but eventually sent it back to the new district superintendent. He could have taught two hundred verses on restitution to me, and it would not have moved me as much as his own personal story of an "unburied hatchet."

What stories will we tell our children or grandchildren? Do we have any? Have we never done anything that required making restitution? After we have made restitution for past wrongs, God often uses these experiences to help us teach others. Perhaps he is having difficulty restoring this discipline to the church because he has so few examples to use.

restitution humbles us

Restitution is perhaps more humbling than any other discipline of the Christian walk. And any time we are humbled and reminded of who and what we are, it is good!

restitution vaccinates us against future wrongs

Nothing can guarantee that we won't slip and fall again, but restitution comes close. The next time we are tempted to take something that doesn't belong to us, we can remember the pain and humiliation of returning to make restitution. When we are about to let loose with biting, sarcastic, hurtful remarks, we may think of the embarrassment in store for us when we later must ask for forgiveness. These thoughts tend to be preventative medicine. A little pain now—doing without or biting the tongue—is preferable to the greater pain of restitution.

how to begin practicing restitution

Doing the right thing the wrong way may make things worse. Just as there is a collective wisdom about how to pray, read the Bible, or restore a backsliding brother or sister, so there is sound, sensible advice on how to make restitution.

start with the key unmade restitution

What is God pointing out to you? Don't try to copy other people's stories. Seek God first. He will impress upon you where you should begin. Seek his face; find out from him where to begin. Don't be discouraged by how many ideas he brings to mind. Simply deal with one offense at a time. Many Christians have felt released by God after they've worked only part way through their list. Turn to God and ask him to tell you where to begin. Then start there.

Perhaps a word of caution is in order about becoming obsessive about restitution. While it is an important discipline of the Christian life, it is not the exclusive one. If you have sought God's guidance, have made a list, and are moving toward settling these past accounts, happily march on your way. God is not an angry ogre in the sky who wants to beat you over the head with your unfinished list. He simply wants you to get moving on the road of obedience.

prepare your speech

Think through what you are going to say. Identify the basic offense. Was it harshness? A critical spirit? Disloyalty? Did you steal something? Would you call it unkindness, vengefulness, or anger? Was it an outburst of rage? Label it clearly with one or two words. Then prepare your speech. Say something like, "I was wrong in my _____ toward you, and I ask you to forgive me. Will you forgive me?" That's it, just a simple statement of confession and request. Anything more and you're liable to cause more problems than you solve.

If you're having trouble saying, "I was wrong," since they were wrong too, remember you are not affirming that they were right. You are simply asking forgiveness for the wrong that you are accountable for. Their wrongdoing is their problem, not yours. So carefully and prayerfully think through what you want to say.

pick the right time, place, and means

Think through the best time to make restitution. Don't talk to the person when he or she is exceptionally busy, tired, or irritable. Generally, the sooner the better, but don't be so hasty that you pick a poor time and place. You should make restitution privately or at least off to the side of a group. And limit the restitution to only the offended party. Restitution needs to be no more public than the sin. In fact, I believe that direct restitution should not be made at all for past sexual sins. Gaining a clear conscience from God and, perhaps, making amends to another person as a representative (such as a minister or counselor) is probably a better plan. But in most cases, direct restitution should be made. A note sometimes works, though seldom for serious matters. A phone call, with the possibility of interchange, is usually better. A face-to-face encounter is often the best means. Use your head, get some advice from a Christian you respect, and do what seems best.

don't combine witnessing with restitution

Simply make your restitution, and get on with life. If the person inquires, answer any questions. Otherwise, don't advertise how spiritual you are now that you have returned to make things right. Restitution is not a soul-winning method. Occasionally, mixing the two will work, but it will usually backfire, ruining both your restitution and your witness.

give a full confession

Come clean. People are always trying to make themselves look better, even while making restitution. For instance, we sometimes say, "You know, I've been thinking of how we were wrong when . . ." This way you both share the blame. Don't implicate anyone else; just say, "I was wrong. Will you forgive me?" Don't say, "I apologize," either. You apologize for minor misunderstandings and comments. When you are wrong say, "I was wrong. Will you forgive me?" It is easy to reduce the seriousness of our offenses. Also, avoid saying, "I'm sorry." Of course you're sorry, and so are they and everyone else that the whole thing happened. Being sorry is not enough. Simply say, "I was wrong. Will you forgive me?"

Perhaps the easiest way to make a partial restitution is to say, "I didn't mean to . . ." When using this phrase, you are really saying, "I'm such a nice person. I would never imagine hurting another creature; my motives were absolutely pure, yet you were still offended, so out of the goodness of my heart, I am coming to confess to you that I didn't mean anything at all." Nonsense! The offended person can't judge your motives. They were offended by your actions, not your motives. So say, "I was wrong. Will you forgive me?"

We rebel against this discipline of restitution. Even after we've decided to do it, there is a tendency for self-protection and pride to creep in. But with some good sense, sound advice, and a commitment to obey Christ in this matter, we can find the happiness of obedient living if we will determine to do it.

restitution lifestyle

Ideally, we're not supposed to be making lists of things we've done in the past. I think God wants us to keep our accounts short. When someone has something against us, we should go and make it right immediately, even if we stand at a sacred altar offering up a holy sacrifice (Matt. 5:23–24). As soon as we sense we have hurt someone, we should return to him or her and make things right. The moment we recognize something we don't own is among our things, we should return it at once. This is a restitution lifestyle—settling accounts immediately. After all, that's when it's easiest.

However, is this restitution lifestyle the ideal? Maybe not. Actually, God's ideal is not needing to make restitution at all. It is making sure we never take things that are not our own. This is the ideal. The idea is growing in maturity to the extent we don't ever say or do anything that hurts other people. This is the ideal.

Certainly, we can never be free from misunderstandings or from having enemies. And we can't be guaranteed that others will even grant their forgiveness. But we do know that we need not be doomed to a life of constant stumbling and falling, regularly doing things that require restitution. God's plan of transformation is far greater than this. To start with, we may need to clean up some past offenses. Then we may need to learn to keep our accounts short through a restitution lifestyle. But eventually, God wants to bring us to the place where we don't need to make restitution because we have completely obeyed Christ.

what about you?

Can you think of any unmade restitutions? Are there things you've taken that were not yours? Are there people you've hurt who have something against you? Do you have a totally clear conscience?

What are your specific plans to practice the discipline of restitution this week?

forgive or not hold it against them.

15. forgiveness

For if you forgive men when they sin against you, your heavenly Father will also forgive you. But if you do not forgive men their sins, your Father will not forgive your sins.

—Matthew 6:14–15

Miss Culp, my third-grade teacher, was a stout woman, about four-and-a-half-feet tall. She led a one-woman crusade to reform education in the city where I grew up. She believed young teachers were too soft on children. Discipline, harshness, and severity were her methods. Remember that this was now many years ago.

I was a special problem for Miss Culp, not because I misbehaved so much, but for other reasons. The first was that I passed into third grade from Miss Hinchman's second-grade room. These two women represented the opposite extremes of educational philosophy. Miss Hinchman's second grade was a womb of positive affirmation. To Miss Hinchman, everything was beautiful, fantastic, lovely, and creative. She believed, "If you expect the best from children, they'll live up to your expectations." On the other hand, Miss Culp subscribed to the theory, "If you give 'em an inch, they'll take a mile." She believed it was her personal calling to straighten out the rascals Miss Hinchman's softness had produced before we turned out to be juvenile delinquents.

But I was a second problem for Miss Culp. It had to do with my dad. On the first day of class, each of us were forced to stand erect, pronounce our name, and tell what our father did for a living. Fearfully, I gave my name and announced that my dad was a preacher. "Hurrumph!" she said. "Preachers' kids are the worst of all. I'll be watching out for you." So Miss Culp expected the worst from me, and I'm afraid she got it.

But there was also a third problem: spelling. Miss Culp gave verbal spelling tests. Each student was sent to the front of the room to stand at attention with "arms straight at your side, fingers pointing to the floor." Miss Culp would move to the back of the classroom, settling down on a large table she kept back there. She would call out spelling words for each student, ordering him or her to spell each word aloud.

I remember my first such experience. "All right young man, spell *elephant*," she announced as if she were making an accusation.

"E-l-e-p-h . . . h . . ."

"Hurry, lad. Finish quickly. You either know it or you don't," she said, with no sympathy for my slowness.

"E-l-e-p-h . . . e-n-t," I quickly finished.

"Wrong," her voice boomed out across the room, with a hint of victory. "No, no, no, that's wrong. Try again."

My heart was beating like a jackhammer. My throat was dry. Blood rushed to my face, and my cheeks turned pink, then red with embarrassment. "E-l-a-p-h-e-n-t," I sputtered out through nervous lips, hoping I might hit it right this time—anything to escape this painful embarrassment and be seated.

"Nooooo!" she said scornfully, "You're spelling it worse every time. What's the matter with you?"

"What *is* the matter with me?" I wondered. Maybe I really was dumb, at least in spelling. I dreaded spelling day every week. Several times I tried feigning an upset stomach to get out of going to school. It seldom worked. Week after week I was subjected to public reproach and Miss Culp's chiding denouncements for my stupidity in spelling.

I don't remember if I ever spelled *elephant* correctly. I do know that I missed most of the words served up to me from her pitcher's mound in the back of the room. I had been so humiliated in my stupidity that I simply decided, "I can't spell." I can still visualize my first red mark on my report card—big, red, indelible ink—a failure in spelling. This failing grade confirmed my dullness.

At first I assumed I was the problem. But later as I realized what she had done to me, I resented her treatment of me. Poor spelling was an ever-present monkey on my back. All through elementary school, high school, and college it was a constant humiliation. I blamed Miss Culp for ruining my attitude about spelling. My resentment grew into a full-blown grudge by high school. Bitterness set in. I never spoke of my third-grade experience to anyone, but I secretly hated Miss Culp for what she had done. "She had no right to treat me that way," I thought.

Funny how a little injustice, if nursed, will grow up to be a full-fledged grudge. I never saw Miss Culp after the fourth grade, but I remembered and resented her. I left her life, but she never left mine. She was constantly haunting me every time I tried to write on a chalkboard or an overhead projector. Worst of all, she was there when I prepared a manuscript for publication. Her memory constantly reminded me of my stupidity in spelling.

Why did she shadow me so? Because of my grudge. Forgive her? Not on your life! "I could never forgive her," I told myself. "She was wrong!"

Sixteen years later, I finally broke free from Miss Culp's dark shadow. I had been elected as my denomination's executive editor of curriculum, a post in which spelling was a necessity. "Why can't I spell?" I asked myself. "Am I really stupid?" God gently reminded me of my buried feelings toward Miss Culp. I was using her as an excuse for my continued failure to spell correctly. I didn't even look up words when unsure. I figured, "Let the assistant look it up. I can't spell anyway."

As God exposed the breadth and depth of my old grudge against Miss Culp, I came to realize its fruitlessness. I hadn't hurt her a bit. In my attempt to even the score with her, I had only hurt myself. The blame for my inability to spell hung as a burden around my neck, not hers. I confessed to a sinful grudge that day and fully forgave Miss Culp. No, I did not say she was a fine teacher, because she wasn't. But I determined that I would no longer hold a grudge against her. It was too costly to me; I fully forgave her.

Following that incident, I went about learning how to spell. In a few years, I caught up. Except when I tell this story, I have almost forgotten about Miss Culp. And now I can spell.

the trouble with grudges

If we slow down and reflect a few moments, each of us will come to admit that a grudge is an awful blot on our souls. What do we gain? Why not release our grudges now? Have you been hurt deeply? Ever? By whom? Has this personal injustice ignited resentment in your heart? Has your resentment turned into a grudge? If so, think about these consequences of grudges.

grudges don't work

When people hurt us, we are inclined to settle the score and get even. If we do not forgive the offenders, the choice remaining is to try revenge or decide to hold a grudge. Revenge is an outward attempt to even the score. A grudge is revenge turned inward. But a grudge doesn't work. The people who hurt us may not even know how angry and bitter we feel. In fact, they may go on their merry way, completely oblivious to our feelings of resentment. They are happy; we are angry, sour, and bitter. The irony is that in getting even with others, we only hurt ourselves spiritually, emotionally, and perhaps even physically.

grudges grow like cancer

Inner resentment is a spreading cancer of the soul. It multiplies its malignant tentacles, spreading to the deepest parts of our hearts. A grudge pours its corrosive bitterness into our entire mind-set. Soon we open the door for envy, malice, jealousy, bitterness, gossip, and slander. We will stop at nothing to even the score. Holding grudges will eat away at our insides. Eventually, we will become bitter people. All this happens because we refuse to forgive those who hurt us. We think the price is too high and that it's not worth it.

grudges generate guilt

If we have grudges but willfully and continually refuse to forgive those who hurt us, we won't feel forgiven ourselves. People who hold grudges seldom sense God is satisfied with them. We will experience free-floating guilt, which attaches itself to all kinds of little things in our lives. We will not be able to put our fingers on it, but for some reason or another, we feel guilty. We think God is mad at us. We will never fully feel forgiven and accepted by God. Why? Because it is a universal law that those who will not forgive do not feel forgiven.

It is not that God makes some sort of deal with us, as if we can buy our forgiveness from him by forgiving others. Jesus Christ has already bought our forgiveness. However, we can inhibit our abilities to sense God's forgiveness by holding grudges. So if we often feel that God has something against us, we may need to look to our pasts. Have we not forgiven someone who has hurt us?

grudges handcuff us to the past

Holding grudges keeps life running on rewind. We keep looking over our shoulders at past injustices we experienced. We recall how awful they were. Grudges handcuff us to this negative past, causing us to blame our present failures on past misfortunes. We think, "If only they hadn't done that, then I'd not be in this jam now."

grudges are energy leaks

The embers of grudges require tending. Resentment left to itself flickers and dies. It must be fed to be kept alive. Where does this fuel come from? It comes from our own mental and emotional energies. Carrying grudges pokes holes in our energy buckets. We will feel constantly tired, weary, and lethargic. Fatigue is the faithful companion of grudges. At the end of each day, we will collapse in exhaustion, wondering why we feel so fatigued. It is because we are wasting great amounts of unconscious energy maintaining our grudges. Releasing these grudges through forgiveness will result in a brand new surge of emotional and physical energy.

This is not to say that everyone who is tired at the end of a hard day's work is harboring a grudge. Weariness is a symptom of an unforgiving spirit, just as a rash is a symptom of poison ivy. All rashes do not indicate poison ivy, but a person infected with poison ivy will have a rash. All exhaustion does not indicate a buried grudge, but if you have a grudge, there is a good chance you'll experience fatigue.

grudges usurp God's rightful role

The ultimate sin in having an unforgiving spirit is that we take God's authority from him. God—and God alone—has the right to condemn men and women. Only God has the right to hold people accountable for their sins. Vengeance is his exclusive domain. When we refuse to forgive others, we raise ourselves to the level of God, as if we can hold others under charges for their sins. Forgiveness allows us to turn this account over to the ultimate Collector of debts.

how to begin practicing forgiveness

All of us recognize the danger of grudges. This leads us to somehow try to remedy the problem. One danger is to choose an insufficient remedy, treating only the surface problem, not the deep resentment within. Consider these inadequate remedies and what *not* to do.

cover it up

You won't escape the clutches of a grudge by simply trying to cover it up. This kind of suppression will only lead to a further poisoning of your spirit. Saying, "I'll pretend it never happened," would be like trying to cure cancer with aspirin. Covering up a grudge with soothing words will only submerge it, allowing it to spread unchecked inside you. Radical surgery is the solution, not aspirin!

forget it

God is not asking you to forget the offense. You simply can't do that. He does, but he does not ask you to do the same. He has designed you so that your memory contains all the events of your life. It is conceivable that you could remember everything that ever occurred in your life. You can especially remember painful experiences or more so the feelings resulting from those experiences. When you fully forgive people, you do not have the capacity to forget their sins. "Forgive and forget" is an ability beyond human capacity.

While you can't forget an offense, you can choose not to dwell on it. When the Devil brings it up again, you can quickly dismiss the event as forgiven. You can't fully erase the memory banks of your mind, and God won't do that for you either. But you do have the power to refuse to think on past injustices once they are forgiven. The curious thing is that once an offense is fully forgiven, the time between you remembering it will increase as time passes. Eventually, months or even years will pass without a thought of this deep hurt. For all practical purposes you might say, "I've forgotten it," though it still lies deep in your memory. The difference is that this file is now marked "forgiven."

excuse it

"But she was wrong," I argued with the Lord about Miss Culp. "If I forgive her, it would be like admitting what she did was OK." No. God doesn't ask me to justify a person's sin, only he can do that. He only asks me to forgive the person. We misunderstand forgiveness. Forgiveness can only be granted if the other person was wrong. But it is only in being wronged that we are empowered to forgive. To forgive Miss Culp, I had to label her actions wrong; I could not excuse them.

God calls us to forgive one another as he forgave us (Col. 3:13). How did God handle your sins? Did he dismiss them with a hasty, "Oh, you needn't worry about your sins; they're minor, and I understand"? No. God forgives us by condemning our sins, then granting a pardon. This is what he asks you to do. Condemn the injustice as wrong, then grant a pardon anyway. Hate the sin, but love the sinner enough to forgive him or her!

what about you?

Have you been hurt? Has someone been unjust to you? Perhaps you've been hurt by a group or institution. Have you fully forgiven these people? Do you harbor a bit of a grudge for anyone anywhere in your past?

If so, you can get this monkey off your back for good today! You can decide that from this moment on, you are marking the debt "paid in full." It is in the decision to forgive that you can actually forgive. You can do it! In one single transaction, you can determine that you will no longer consider that your offender has an outstanding balance with you. The debt is history, cancelled, paid in full, turned over to the Eternal Debt Collector, not because the person was right, but simply because you want to obey Christ and please him. He has commanded you to forgive others as he has forgiven you—completely, wholly, irrevocably. Can you do the same for another now? It's not a question of *who* is right; it's a question of *what* is right.

Perhaps your injury was especially deep. Could you at least begin to forgive? Are you telling yourself, "I can't forgive," when you really mean, "I won't forgive"? Are you truly unable to forgive? Are you willing to be made willing? Is the Lord gently urging you to begin? If so, why not turn the corner today? Why not tell him right now, "Lord, I'm going to begin my road to recovery, and I will not turn back until I have fully forgiven that person"? The Great Forgiver will help you.

What are your specific plans to practice the discipline of forgiveness this week?

16. capturing thoughts

We take captive every thought to make it obedient to Christ.
—2 Corinthians 10:5

We live in a sex-saturated society. Advertisers use sex appeal to sell perfume, shave lotion, blue jeans, hosiery, even toothpaste. Most of the TV advertising we see is carefully designed to appeal to our sensual natures. A modern diet cola advertisement is quite as erotic as many adult magazines of a few decades ago. Magazines, books, newspapers, billboards, movies, and even office conversations offer stimulation of the sexual parts of our beings. An increasing host of soft-core TV programs titillate millions of viewers every night, and what was once considered blatantly sexy is now accepted as good taste in clothing.

Is it any wonder that believers living in such a society are troubled by improper sexual thoughts? The temptation to dwell on sexual themes and erotic thoughts is everywhere.

Impure thoughts are not a temptation limited to only young men. I once thought this to be so, but experience in counseling for many years has taught me otherwise. I have talked with many older men plagued with this private sin and have suffered for forty or fifty years since their teens. Lust is also not exclusively a sin of men. My wife reports from her traveling and speaking schedule that she has counseled innumerable women, young and old alike, who suffer with habitual sexual fantasies.

If this area of temptation is completely foreign to you or if you are aghast that there are Christians who wrestle with this awful demon, the following excerpts from two letters may be helpful in describing the depth of this particular fleshly sin.

I'm desperate for any help you can give me. I am so sick of my obsession with impure thoughts that I have thought of suicide. I feel so filthy, so dirty, so unworthy after I've given in and dwelled on some memory or daydream about a beautiful woman. My guilt brings me to confess. And I promise God I'll never do it again. But I do. I always do. Sometimes I fight. Sometimes I even beat this monster, but I often fall. *Very* often.

Is there any help for me? Am I too far gone? Should I simply give up at trying to be a Christian? That's how I feel sometimes. This filthy habit has clung to my life for more than thirty years. I've never told anybody else about it. My pastor, the board, the whole church—even my wife— all think I am a perfect model Christian. But I know I am rotten inside. I feel like such a hypocrite! Is there hope for me? If so, I need it soon.

Or consider this letter my wife received from a delightfully talented woman.

I had never even thought of how women have impure thoughts until last week at your session. I always figured guys were the ones who had problems with "dirty thoughts." But maybe I have a problem too.

There's this handsome young man in our church choir who is not only talented, but pays attention to me. My husband is one of those guys who pretty well ignores me, especially in public. But this guy treats me like a queen. He listens to what I have to say, looks right into my face, and acts like I'm an important person. You know what I mean—he just treats me *special*.

I wonder if this has become a trap for me. I think about him all the time—while I'm working, during church services, even when I'm with my husband. Not that I think of having sex with this man or anything like that. I just invent those intensely romantic scenes in my mind, as if they are happening between him and me. It's exciting! But I wonder if it's wrong. Is it OK as long as I don't fantasize about the actual sex act?

All of this has made a big difference in how I feel about myself lately. I now have something to get up for in the morning again. Even my husband complimented me recently (believe it or not!) on how nicely I've been dressing. Could these thoughts be wrong when they seem to have so many benefits?

What would you tell this woman? What would you tell that man in the first letter?

what is lust?

Some spiritual advisors are not worried by these kinds of thoughts. They soothe troubled Christians by saying that sexual fantasies are common, normal, and quite innocent. A few even consider impure thoughts as healthy for a marriage.

The Bible is not so soft on this issue. It names such thoughts with one word: *lust*. God's Word condemns lust as sin. Christians are to get rid of it along with other evil thoughts, words, and actions. Fooling around with lust is like playing with a loaded gun. Given the chance, impure thoughts will ruin your soul. Lust is serious. Jesus shocked his audience by stating that in God's sight, lust is as serious as adultery itself (see Matt. 5:27–29).

So, what is lust? It is dwelling on sexual thoughts that, if we carried them out in real life, would clearly be sin. Lust is sexual or sensual fantasies about someone we are not married to. Lust is sinful sexual passion. It is sinful sexual thinking nurtured in our minds and dwelled on for the sake of personal sensual pleasure. Lust is willfully and purposefully thinking these thoughts.

Those blessed with high sexual energy may be especially tempted in this area. Satan may frequently bring a memory to mind, tempting us to dwell on it. Or he may attempt to seduce us to fantasize about a particular person. This is not lust; it is temptation. While it is sometimes difficult for us to determine the fine line between disobedience and temptation, there is a world of difference between an evil thought and the thought of evil. Even Jesus had thoughts of evil while he was not guilty of evil thoughts. He banished these thoughts from his mind with a decisive refusal to surrender, and a quote from God's Word (see Matt. 4:1–11). Lust is not only temptation; it is surrendering to temptation, dwelling on the impure thoughts Satan has presented to our minds.

Lustful dreaming in not sinful either. Dreams are a mysterious function in our subconscious minds. Have you ever dreamed that you shot and killed someone? I have. I woke up trembling and *felt* as if I had actually committed murder. But I was not guilty of murder, even in God's sight. God does not hold us accountable for the mysterious working of our subconscious minds. Dreaming is not sin; *daydreaming* is the problem. Lust is purposefully dwelling on sinful, sensual thoughts. These are the wild horses of our minds that must be tracked down, captured, and made obedient to Christ.

the trouble with impure thoughts

justifying sin

The Great Deceiver tells us, "Don't worry about these thoughts; they're harmless, innocent fantasies." He would like us to dismiss them as the ordinary musings of all humanity. This sometimes works for him. The human mind cannot survive long when our behaviors are out of sync with our beliefs. If we believe something is wrong, we will want to stop it. However, if we fail at our attempts to stop, we will then try to rationalize the thought, word, or action. We justify it as appropriate, thus escaping the tension of doing what we know we shouldn't. If we do not beat this thing, we will eventually justify lust as ordinary and inescapable.

living a double life

If we are truly saved, the Holy Spirit won't abandon his convicting work. Though we tell ourselves this sin is OK, the Holy Spirit will keep telling us otherwise. We will then adopt a new strategy: partitioning life like a rolltop desk. We decide to simply ignore this part of our lives. We create a pigeonhole for impure thoughts and pretend they don't exist.

Churches are full of men and women who live this kind of double life. They tuck their evil thoughts into a sealed desk drawer of their minds. Into this drawer they enter alone. These people seem quite ordinary when you meet them, work with them, or serve on a committee with them. But they are Jekyll-and-Hyde Christians. Though they grow in other areas, appearing to make progress along the highway of holiness, they have a cancerous closet in their minds. These double-minded Christians sneak off to dwell on corrupt and sordid thoughts, then cower back full of guilt and despair. This is a wretched way to live.

having unquenchable thirst

Sexual pursuits outside marriage are like an empty well. They promise satisfaction but leave us unfulfilled. The more we dwell on these thoughts, the less exciting they will be for us. In our quests for fulfillment, we will be on a perpetual treadmill of self-gratification. The faster we chase satisfaction, the less satisfied we will be. Like drinking salt water, the more we drink, the less our thirst is quenched.

becoming obsessed

Sexual fantasies are addictive. Once we establish the habit, we will begin a relentless cycle of obsession. These thoughts will gradually permeate every recess of our minds. They will dominate us, enslaving us in the bondage of despair. Eventually, our entire lives will be tarnished by them. We will be hooked on the opium of sexual fantasies. We will be obsessed with the quest for satisfaction—always hungering, never satisfied. We will be slaves to lust.

diverting wholesome sexual energy

The Devil didn't invent sex; God did. He termed it "good" along with the rest of creation. The most important sex organ in the body is the mind. God designed our minds with the powerful capacity to direct and focus sexual energy toward another. This remarkable mental ability is God-given and designed to produce the great sexual satisfaction in marriage. This God-given ability should be focused on our spouses, not squandered on some fleeting fantasy. When we surrender to impure thoughts, we poke a leak in our own sexual energies, which ultimately produces frustration and unfulfillment.

changing thoughts to action

On this one concept, philosophers and great thinkers throughout history agree: As we think, we shall become. If we think positive, uplifting, wholesome, healthy thoughts, we will eventually become positive, uplifting, wholesome, healthy people. If we think gloomy, negative, sickly thoughts, we will turn out to be gloomy, negative, sickly people. What we think, we become. As the Bible says, "As he thinketh in his heart, so is he" (Prov. 23:7 KJV).

Our minds are like fertile fields. The field doesn't care what is planted in it. It simply obeys the universal law: What is planted in the field will grow abundantly. If we plant corn, we'll get corn. Likewise, our thoughts are seeds. What we plant will sprout and grow, eventually producing an abundant crop in real life.

Can we see the ultimate results of impure thinking? "Innocent fantasies" planted in our minds will eventually produce abundant crops of sinful behavior. What we thought were benign mental pastimes carried on in the privacy of our minds will turn out to be the doorways through which our moral downfall enters. Thoughts lead to actions. Our sensual thought lives will not escape this universal law of life. Sooner or later, we will act as we think.

how to begin practicing taking thoughts captive

If you have been enslaved by impure thoughts, there is good news for you. You can be completely free! If you seriously hunger to be free from the bondage of impure thoughts, God is able to do it. These ideas are not some philosophy dreamed up in an ivory tower of theory. Rather, they have been hammered out in the trenches of life by hundreds of men and women who once suffered in defeat but are now free of this clinging sin.

confess

All improvement starts with confession. Quit dismissing impure thoughts as inconsequential. Tear down the partition to that private closet in your mind, allowing Christ's light to expose these thoughts of darkness. Call them what God does: lust. Agree with God concerning this sin and begin your journey to a pure mind.

expose lust's big lie

Admit to yourself and to God that this way of life does not bring ultimate satisfaction. Acknowledge that the promises of the Deceiver are lies. Lust is not satisfying; it never has been and never will be. Keep reminding yourself that the Devil is a liar from the beginning. Start remembering where all this daydreaming could eventually lead—to sinful behavior, moral collapse, and maybe the breakup of your home.

starve the sources

Track down your stimuli and get tough with them! What is it that gets your mind going? Is it the story section of a women's magazine? Is it a particular TV program? Movies? Soap operas? Music? Is it a certain person who is flirting with you? Is it making jokes soaked in double entendres? Certain websites? Do romance novels start your sexual engines? Is it indecent jokes or stories of another's sexual activities? What is the outside source of your temptation?

Your mind is fearfully and wonderfully made. It is incredible. Better than the best computer, the mind is constantly receiving messages, processing input, and affecting your behavior. When you expose your mind to stimuli, it affects what you think. If your mind is wandering into sexual fantasies, somewhere along the line it has received stimuli which triggered these thoughts. Track down and avoid your besetting stimuli.

Lust is a hungry carnivorous monster. It must be fed "flesh" to survive. External stimuli triggers lust. These stimuli continuously nourish and multiply a lustful orientation. Since society is saturated with sexual stimuli, you may be tempted to play along, to simply give up. But you need not do this. With a little thought, you could make a list of the ten most dangerous triggers for temptation in this area. Then starve the sources.

win with the Word

How will you keep from sinning against God? By hiding God's Word in your heart. A consistent habit of reading, memorizing, and meditating on God's Word is incompatible with impure thoughts. One will eventually destroy the other. Which one wins in your life?

Believers who are failing to live above impure thoughts will almost always confess they are not practicing a regular habit of systematic devotional Bible reading. The road to pure thoughts always runs through Scripture. The most important habit you can begin to aid in your battle against temptation is time alone with God every day. If the Devil is tempting you to lustful thoughts, start with these Scriptures:

Ps 73:26

- Psalm 13:2
- Psalm 19:13–14
- Psalm 119:9–11
- Proverbs 2:12–19
- Proverbs 5:1–23
- Proverbs 6:24–29
- Proverbs 7:1–27
- 1 Corinthians 6:18–20
- 1 Corinthians 10:13

- 2 Corinthians 10:5
- Galatians 5:24–25
- Philippians 4:7
- Colossians 3:2–7
- 1 Timothy 4:12
- 1 Timothy 5:2
- 2 Timothy 2:22
- Hebrews 3:1
- James 1:14–15

Temptation & thoughts on Jesus. Can lead to downfall

practice displacement

If you have ample amounts of unoccupied time, you will be a sitting duck for Satan. If you are often alone, you may find Satan coming in like a flood during these times. Perhaps your job is boring and unchallenging, allowing time for your mind to wander and wonder. When a mind is unoccupied, the Devil takes this opportunity to suggest sinful thoughts for you to dwell on.

Displacement is concentrating your mental energies on other things. It is filling your mind with other thoughts, focusing your mental powers elsewhere. Impure thoughts are crowded out. Search for a mental infatuation with something else: Scripture memorization, baseball, an invention you're working on, taking a class at a nearby college, a new floor plan for your dream house. Anything decent will do. Find something that can occupy your mind, and displace impure thoughts.

redirect your thoughts

If you are married, you already have discovered that the temptation to think impure thoughts does not go away after the wedding. In some ways, the amount of these thoughts increases. But the married person has one definite counterforce against this temptation: When you are tempted to think sexual thoughts, go ahead and think them. Rather than developing a negative obsession about these thoughts, redirect them properly toward your spouse. Use your sexual thoughts to enhance your own sex life in marriage; focus your thoughts toward that relationship where sexual expression is beautiful and God-sanctified. This is the wholesome use of your powerful mental sexual energies.

drink from your own spring

If you are married, work on developing a satisfying sexual relationship at home. Developing a sexual relationship takes tenderness, understanding, patience, and hard work. Learn to flirt with each other again. Recapture the tremendous sexual power of a meaningful glance. Practice romance. Surprise him. Allure her. Keep the fire hot at home.

turn temptation into spiritual energy

Do a turnabout on the Devil. When he introduces some delectable temptation to you, immediately go to prayer. Not for yourself, but for others. Take your temptation as a signal that Satan would love to have you fall so that he can more easily get to those in your circle of influence. What about your son? Daughter? Spouse? Congregation? People in your church? Someone you mentor? Could they be tempted likewise? Most likely they are, so go to prayer for them, asking that they will be strong in their similar temptation. This is a great trick to play on Satan. His temptation merely sends you to earnest prayer for others. The more he tempts you, the more you pray.

become accountable

You will never overcome having impure thoughts on your own. Find someone of the same sex whom you trust, preferably someone who has fought a similar battle and won. Ask him or her to check up on your thought life every time he or she sees you. Make sure your accountability partner is tough on you, never satisfied with less than 100 percent purity.

seek deliverance

If you carefully follow each of the above prescriptions, you will find great victories and progress in your struggle. You will become an overcomer most of the time. You may say, "I've come a long way," but you may not be completely free. You will still yearn for complete freedom. You will want more than partial victory. You will not even be satisfied with 100 percent "victory." You will want deliverance (see Rom. 7:4–25; 8:2–3). You can have it. God carries deliverance in stock. You can do more than fight the battle, often winning, sometimes losing. You can do more than resist the magnetic pull of the flesh.

True, you will likely not ever be totally delivered from temptation in this area (or at least related areas). But you need not fall. You need not be content with being a recovering lustaholic. You can have deliverance. You'll never completely beat this thing through striving, though strive you must. You'll never defeat this clinging habit through hard work, though work you must. Only Jesus can bind this evil spirit of the mind. It is only the Son of God who can drive these thieves from the temple of your heart. God can deliver you. And he will if you let him.

Now don't leap too quickly at this opportunity for a short-cut. Don't say to yourself, "Good, I'll seek instant deliverance. It's certainly easier than memorizing these Scriptures." God will see through your shallowness and spiritual laziness. He expects you to work. And as you work, so will he. As you pursue a healthy and pure thought life, also seek his total deliverance. He can do it! It could happen today or after months or even years of seeking. It could happen gradually or in a single instant. But it can happen. There is not one sin that you cannot be free of. God forgives; he also delivers. Let it happen.

what about you?

Do you suffer defeat in your thought life? Has lust plagued you for years? Have you almost given up hope of being free of this beast? Don't give in. Don't give up. Rather, cheer up! Look up! Your hope of deliverance is near. If God's gentle Spirit convicts you of this sin, rejoice, because he never convicts without the hope of correction. Your conviction is cause for joy! There is hope. Beginning today, you can be free!

What are your specific plans to practice the discipline of taking thoughts captive this week?

17. restoration

*If someone is caught in a sin, you who are spiritual should restore
him gently. But watch yourself, or you also may be tempted.*

—Galatians 6:1

Suppose someone has taken a spiritual tumble in your church.
He has fallen into sin, and many know about it. A little group
gathers off to the side to discuss the tragedy. One opens the
conversation with, "Isn't it just terrible? Of all people, who
would ever have suspected *him*?" Another replies, "He should
have known better. It was just plain stupid." A third adds,
"We've got to raise up the whole family in prayer during this
time; you know this was not the *first* time."

So go the unspiritual, fleshly responses to a believer's fall into
sin. We have a difficult time dealing with a brother or sister's
spiritual failure in the Christian community. If a leader or minister
falls, the difficulty is doubled. What is a congregation to do
when one of its own falls?

What if one of our unmarried teens gets pregnant? Or how should we respond when one of the board members is being charged with tax evasion in his business? Or how about a fine fellow in our choir who is being charged by his former wife for molesting his children? What do we do when one of our adult Sunday school teachers separates from his wife and files for a no-fault divorce? What would you do if you caught another Christian secretly meeting with someone who is not his or her spouse?

Sometimes Christians fall into sin. It is not the norm and should not be expected, but it happens. Christians sometimes stumble and fall. Temptation, like a mighty gust of wind, can sweep believers off their feet and send them tumbling. When this happens, what should the rest of us do? We are to restore our fallen brothers and sisters. We are to help them back on their feet again. This discipline is both personal and corporate—the individual has a responsibility as does the entire church. We are commanded to help them up. This is restoration.

what not to do when a believer falls

Restoring another Christian is a demanding responsibility and can be a sensitive task. How will the person respond? Will the person blow up at us? Is the whole thing merely a rumor that we should ignore? It's none of our business anyway, is it? It is indeed our responsibility. God wants to restore the fallen one, and he chooses to use us as his helpers and restorers. The responsibility for restoration lies squarely on the shoulders of other Christians. But because of misunderstanding, fear, and lack of training, we often sidestep this command. Rather, we bypass the whole issue when faced with another's sin.

we must not whitewash sin

Excusing sin as normal or ordinary doesn't help. "After all, he's only human," we say, apparently believing it is simply natural for Christians to fall into sin. Some churches have used the guise of "loving the sinner" to completely ignore the commands of the Scripture. Yes, we must love sinners, even when they are fallen brothers or sisters, but we are not to dismiss their sins with trivial remarks about humanity, treating sin as inconsequential. Jesus told one sinner, "Neither do I condemn you," but he quickly added, "Go now and leave your life of sin" (John 8:11).

Like a disease, sin spreads its influence. It is contagious, spreading from one to another. We are called to restore our fallen brothers and sisters, not merely excuse them. Whitewashing sin by excusing it as human error bypasses the whole issue, ignores God's command to restore fallen believers, and gives would-be restorers an easy out from a tough task.

we must not go on a witch hunt

The trouble with this Christian discipline of restoration is that those least likely to do it are usually best for the job. Conversely, those most likely to gleefully greet the idea of restoring others are the worst ones to do it. In most churches, there are a few people who would love the idea of signing up for search-and-destroy missions to uncover and correct the sins of others. They are experts at exposing and condemning sin. These people love nothing better than the juicy discovery of people's wrongdoing. They have what John Calvin called the "spirit of accusation." Like the Pharisees, they are always anxious to cast the first stone. If given their way, they'd return to the days of Salem,

Massachusetts, and sensational church trials, placing offenders in stocks or hanging them as witches. Obviously, this kind of witch-hunt atmosphere is not what restoration is all about.

we must not ignore sin

While most churches may have a witch hunter or two, most of us are in little danger of such excesses. But we are just as guilty. In our attempts to avoid the excesses, we may do worse by simply ignoring the situation altogether, hoping it will go away. We attribute the sin to an exaggerated rumor, saying, "It's probably not true anyway." We remain coldly aloof from the sin and the fallen person, figuring it will evaporate with time. "It's none of our business anyway," we say, hoping that the fallen believer will find a way to heal or fade away.

If you had an ugly, festering wound on your leg with nasty, red lines creeping up toward your heart, would you ignore it? No. When one of the members in the body of Christ is infected with sin, the rest of us must take action to bring healing, not casually stand by in indifference. Ignoring sin won't make it go away. We are to get involved, take a risk, and help where we can. That's what being a Christian is all about. The local church is a hospital for sinners, not a musty museum for perfect saints.

we must not practice shunning

In many churches, offending members are neither restored nor expelled; they are simply given the cold shoulder. They are not officially ignored or rejected, but treated with icy politeness. And there is a dark thing happening—these brothers and sisters, while still present, are quietly being excluded from true fellowship. All interchange is mechanical and automatic. This ostracism is some-what like the shunning practiced by the Amish and other strict sects. We are no better. The people guilty of moral failure never hear their sin spoken of. They are politely greeted and civilly treated, but never again included in anything. It is social excommunication.

Most persons who experience this kind of psychological tor-ture eventually drop out of the church or switch to another fel-lowship that seems more open and accepting. In fact, in almost every community, there are churches that, like the cities of refuge in Israel, are known to provide loving relief and asylum for hurting people. Word gets around. Is your church such a community of the compassionate?

how to begin practicing restoration

The Bible is so intensely practical. It is more than a book of theological ideas we are asked to believe. Rather, it is a guidebook for everyday life. The Book tells us specifically what to do when believers stumble into sin. We are to *restore* them. This same word is used for mending nets or for a surgeon setting a broken bone. Restoration means becoming a repairperson. We are to be involved in helping Christians get to their feet again, putting them back where they belong.

someone must face the offender

Restoration is face-to-face work. It should not be done by let-ter or over the phone. The Bible tells us this is work for the spir-itual ones among our congregations. It's work for mature Christians. Novices and carnal Christians need not apply. Restorers must pick a time and place to face brothers and sisters with the intention to restore. Many churches leave this work to the pastor; the Scriptures don't. Restoration is a Christian discipline that all who are spiritual should bear.

Restoration is delicate work. Restorers are attempting to correct the trajectory of brothers or sisters who have wandered off. It is not to be done without much prayer and thought. Perhaps this is why so few do it. But if you take the Bible seriously, you who are spiritual, mature, and guided by the Spirit are to set up a meeting face-to-face with the person who has fallen.

your spirit must be right

Restorers must approach brothers or sisters in a spirit of meekness, vividly remembering that they too have feet of clay. They must avoid gossip and keep their talking and advice to a minimum. Restoring is not lecture-giving. Godly restorers put the best construction on the actions and motives of the fallen brother or sister. They are not looking for an opportunity to give harsh, heavy-handed condemnation or to illustrate their own spiritual superiority. They are not accusatory or have holier-than-thou attitudes. They are sympathetic and tactful, carefully selecting their words.

Most of all, restorers are humble. Restoration is not the work for those with a spiritual superiority complex. Godly restorers come, not as ones stooping down to raise up another to their level. Rather, they come alongside as friends to help brothers and sisters back to their feet. Restorers are meek people—a blend of strength and tenderness—strong enough to set the broken bone, yet gentle enough to avoid hurting the patient more than necessary as they do it.

There are precious few people who meet these criteria. In fact, merely reading the description may cause you to give up. "Obviously this is not the kind of work for me," you might say to yourself. "I'll pray while others do this restoring business." But don't be too hasty in dismissing the power of the Holy Spirit in your life.

Do you *want* to be this way? Is it your hunger? Can you see a glimmer of hope that you might someday become this sort of a restorer? If so, then let God work in you. If he lays it on your heart to help some slipping (or slipped) saint, then do so without delay. You may discover hidden, untapped characteristics for being just this kind of person. Anyway, how will you know if you never try?

the goal is recovery

Restoring is about discipline, not punishment. Punishment looks backward to the offense and seeks to inflict pain; discipline looks forward toward recovery. Restoring is discipline, and it puts people back on course and gets them moving in the right direction again. You do not visit your brothers and sisters to see them cower in pain and guilt. You want to get the confession out of the way as quickly as possible so you can get on with bringing the cure.

determine your approach

Before you restore, determine what your approach will be. Are you offering simple words to admonish, a more definite correction, or clear-cut rebuke? Each person and each situation may require a different approach. In most cases, give gentle admonition saying something like, "What I want to talk to you about is _____. I don't know for sure, and I could be wrong, but I want to offer a gentle nudge to you, as my friend, about _____. If I'm wrong, forget it and forgive my intrusion. If I'm partly right, then think about it. Kick it around a bit, and see if God is saying the same thing."

There is seldom a need to be harsher than this. In some instances, a more direct correction or outright rebuke is required, but a gentle admonition given early is often adequate.

the means to recovery is repentance

When a Christian falls, there is only one way back—repentance. Repentance is sorrow, brokenness, and heartache for sin. It begins with a confession, but leads to a desire to abandon the sin. When a Christian falls, he or she experiences plenty of guilt and remorse and is usually ready to repent. He or she may have even already repented privately.

That is why it is so important to carefully approach a fallen friend at the most appropriate time. God may already be preparing his or her heart to receive the word of correction. Restorers never arrive first; the Holy Spirit does.

Occasionally, however, people will not receive the correction at all. Sometimes they will deny everything, even attack you. They may dismiss it as a minor offense, tell you it has been exaggerated, or offer excuses for the behavior. Sometimes this happens even after you have done everything right. If it does, simply offer an apology for offending them and change the subject. Dismiss the issue, and treat them tenderly and carefully. Remember, fallen Christians have a serious spiritual wound. Sometimes when you offer therapy, it causes greater pain than the wound itself. In these cases, simply withdraw, and let the Holy Spirit continue his work.

Immediate rejection, however, may be only a temporary delay. Sometimes your admonition is rejected only to become a seed for eventual obedience. The following from a letter illustrates just such a response.

I've always had a good marriage, or at least I thought so. But last year at camp I made the acquaintance of a woman serving on staff with me. My wife was home with our kids, and this woman and I struck up a friendship. We shared lots of interests and liked to talk with each other. Her friendly response to me was a powerful ego stimulant, and we were frequently seen together.

Two of my friends noticed and worried about the direction this friendship was going. They cared enough to talk to me directly about it.

I was furious! How could they suspect anything? What kind of friends were these? *They* were the ones with the dirty minds, not me. And I told them so.

But inwardly the Holy Spirit immediately convicted me. We hadn't done anything wrong, but I was captivated by this woman, and the relationship was headed the wrong way. I argued with God, insisting that he was wrong. I swore that if it ever went further, I'd break it off. I even spoke to the woman about it.

Anyway, after a long period of very deep conviction, I abandoned that relationship, which was headed for trouble. I began pouring my energies into my own marriage. As I did, I was astounded at the dry rot in my own marriage. It wasn't as secure as I'd thought.

To make a long story short, I am now finally able to look back over the past year with joy. My marriage has never been better. I see real growth in myself and my relationship with my wife.

I just want to give credit to those two guys who took such a big risk that day. If they hadn't offered that correction, who knows where that relationship might have led? I think I know. And I thank them for the correction.

Restoration is risky. But where there is no risk, there is no gain. Likewise, where the risk is high, the gains are correspondingly high.

full restoration must come

The whole purpose of restoration is to get people back to where they were, and often that means leadership roles. Why is it that the church will take infamous sinners who have been saved out of the raw and propel them to leadership, while fallen Christians forever forfeit any claim to leadership? It's a kind of Protestant penance, only worse—it never ends. Eventually, fallen Christians who clearly repent and reform should be restored completely, even to leadership.

That doesn't mean such restoration should be immediate, and it doesn't mean that following a hasty repentance, fallen Christians keep all their responsibilities in the church, as if nothing ever happened. On the contrary, Christians who fall into obvious public sin should relinquish all leadership positions in the church, but this should only be for a set time. They should be placed under a loving spiritual mentor for accountability and growth. When a reasonable time has passed, they should be free to be appointed or elected to any post in the church. The immediate need of fallen Christians is restoration to fellowship, not restoration to leadership.

what about you?

Have you ever slipped off the straight-and-narrow path of obedience? Did Satan ever sneak up on your blind side and trip you up, sending you headlong into sin? Was there a time when you found yourself entangled in a habit, thought pattern, or attitude which you couldn't seem to shake? Were you ever knocked over and swept away in an act of disobedience?

How did you want to be treated? With searing judgment and condemnation? Would you have been happy to have been simply ignored and left alone to work it out yourself? Perhaps this is exactly what happened. Wouldn't it have been better if someone who loved you had come to you with a tender and compassionate heart and carefully helped you back on track?

Has anyone ever restored you? God has. We have all been restored by the gentle, strong arm of God. Most of us, many times. Now we who are restored are to become restorers. We who have known disobedience ourselves now become God's instruments to restore other fellow travelers. It's the Christian way.

What are your specific plans to practice the discipline of restoration this week?

18. humility

Pride goes before destruction, a haughty spirit before a fall.
—Proverbs 16:18

Pride is a sinful attitude of superiority with a long growing season. If we are prideful, others will sense it and come to dislike us. Eventually, we will see it ourselves.

Pride sneaks up on us. Several years ago, I was traveling extensively on a speaking circuit. I flew someplace almost every week. It was physically tiring but emotionally exhilarating. I enjoyed being used by the Lord in so many different cultures and among a variety of age groups.

As a souvenir of these trips, I decided to keep the baggage tag hooked on the handle of my suitcase. On retrieving my suitcase after each trip, I tore off the tag and left the string tied around the handle. Over the years, an impressive cluster of strings built up until it looked like a massive carnation. I used it as a prayer reminder—to remember God's faithfulness in providing safe travel to me over the years.

But it also had an effect on others. Being younger than most speakers, I had always faced the attitude that I was a rookie who was getting a good break to be invited to speak. Interestingly enough, as my baggage tags grew and bloomed, this attitude rapidly disappeared. Invariably, the individual who picked me up would be impressed at how much I had traveled. I was impressed too but hardly noticed it.

Then one day as I checked my bag for yet another flight, an enterprising counter clerk produced a knife and offered to cut away the old strings. "I like them there. They're souvenirs," I protested. He shrugged his shoulders and checked the bag through to wherever I was going. But as I walked to the gate, God's quiet voice spoke: "Why do you really want those baggage strings on your bag? Is it really for a prayer reminder or has it become something to impress others?" Throughout the entire flight, I pondered God's questions. Yes, I had to confess to pride. I had allowed Satan to take my simple collecting practice and twist it into a proud attitude. Before the flight ended, I confessed to my pride and repented. I turned away from the behavior. When I got to my hotel room that day, I tore off those strings from my suitcase, one by one, and dropped them into the wastebasket. Pride had quietly found a hiding place among my souvenir baggage tags—actually, in my heart.

Some might say I was too sensitive. But I know pride when I am confronted with it. That is what's so funny about pride: We can sense it in others long before we see it in ourselves.

what is pride?

Pride is thinking more highly of ourselves than we should. It is an inaccurate overestimation of our accomplishments. Self-esteem, even self-love, is good for us. Pride, an overabundance of self-appreciation, is sin. It is a corruption of the essential self-love God expects us to have.

Pride may be the most deceitful of all sins, tucked deep within us, masked in a thousand ways. It has a treacherous influence on other attitudes. Worse than blending with our vices, pride fuses with our virtues. The further along we are in our spiritual walks, the more likely we are to encounter the monster of pride. When we have overcome outward sins, even found victory over sinful inner attitudes and thoughts, Satan unleashes this secret weapon. No longer can he easily drag us away into outward sin. Perhaps now Satan is often beat when attempting to entice us into inner sins like wrong thoughts and attitudes, so he begins to flatter us. Satan reminds us how spiritually minded we are, how far we have come, how much further along we are than many others. And we begin to believe him. Soon devilish spiritual pride mates with our spirits and produces a litter of other sins. Pride tends to mix with both vices and virtues.

acceptable pride

We are not talking here about justifiable pride, the sensible appreciation of fine work or craftsmanship. Obedient Christians might take pride in their city, church, lawn, or children (more so, grandchildren). These are usually reasonable levels of gratification in how things are turning out. If we are going to buy a handmade cabinet or chest, we will want a carpenter who takes pride in his or her work. This kind of dignity in a job well done is expected of a worker worthy of his or her hire.

Just as there is such a thing as righteous anger, so there is righteous pride, a sense of legitimate satisfaction. The apostle Paul was proud of the Corinthian church's response after his first letter to them, and he said so. However, like righteous anger, justifiable pride is a slippery slope. The human spirit tends to justify sin. I sat in a Sunday school class in Pennsylvania where they were discussing how to tell the difference between justifiable pride and sinful pride. One fellow concluded the discussion with, "That's easy: *your* pride is sin; *mine's* justifiable." His comment was greeted with laughter, then the teacher moved on to the next verse.

It is too often true. We can easily rationalize our own pride while condemning it in others. So while we can accept a certain level of self-respect, dignity in work, and satisfaction in others, we must always be aware that even this healthy pride can turn sour, self-serving, and sinful.

what causes pride?

Pride is so universal that it seems not to be the result of cause and effect. It appears to be stamped on the essential nature of humanity. However, there are some conditions that enhance the breeding environment so that pride is more easily cultured. These factors tend to cultivate pride. If one or more are descriptive of our lives, we may need to be on guard against this sin.

success

Once we have achieved success, we tend to take credit for it. Others encourage us to do this. Once we've "made it," everyone assumes we know the secret of success. We are showered with admiration, applause, and invitations to share the secrets that made us successful. Others hungering to succeed listen intently, take notes, and supply generous amounts of flattery. We've made it. After all, we *must* be smarter than everybody else, right? The more success, the greater the temptation to be prideful. We eventually may come to believe all the praise.

knowledge

If pride lives in our hearts, the more we know, the dumber everyone else will appear to be. Being experts in one field can make it difficult to put up with the ignorance around us. It's easy to forget that everything we know, we once had to learn. Intellectual arrogance shows no pity on the unlearned; it is impatient with "common" people.

That is not to say that we should avoid learning (any more than we should avoid success). Success and the ability to learn are gifts of God to be accepted with gratitude; however, as with all gifts, they can also become curses. The dark side of knowledge is the tendency to be prideful. "Knowledge puffs up" (1 Cor. 8:1). The most dangerous fool of all is the college sophomore who became a know-it-all in two quick years of college. Those who truly pursue knowledge eventually discover how little they know.

wealth

Many proud people are not wealthy, but few wealthy people are not proud. The prestige, power, influential position, and possessions of the rich naturally promote pride. Fine clothing, expensive automobiles, and the exquisitely decorated homes of the rich all join together in harmony to laud the importance of the Evil One commanding it all.

creativity

What a gift from God, yet a tool of Satan! The irony is the more talented and creative we are, the more likely we are to see how things "ought to be done." There are some people who could do just about any job they wanted, at church or work, and they could do it better than most anyone else. They simply know how to do things—everything—well.

The danger of creativity is arrogance. Assuming that all others are morons, we offer them our answers to all problems. We have the solutions for our workplaces, churches, denominations, and countries. People nod and listen, seldom arguing with us, because we probably *are* right. But they resent us for it. We are marked as cocky know-it-alls. Our spirits ooze conceit. Unless our talents and creativity are harnessed and directed into proper channels, we will wind up on the sidelines of life, evaluating everything from our own superior perspectives. We may be right, but eventually we'll have no one to tell. All will avoid us like the plague. We will have become arrogant.

talent

The better we are at something, the greater the danger of pride. In what areas do we have talent? Is our talent natural or acquired? Is it music? Art? Athletics? Academics? Leadership? Is there some area where we seem to have natural talent? If so, the tendency is to elevate ourselves, as if we are somehow better than others and this talent is the evidence of it.

virtue

In what way could goodness be a breeding ground of pride? The better we are, the filthier our temptations. When we have achieved spiritual success, we may become a target of the most contemptible pride of all—spiritual pride. With spiritual achievement, pride slithers in. We are tempted to pour contempt on all others who have not come as far as us. We seem so spiritual: "And these others, these carnal Christians, why, they are so shallow and simple. If only they could grow up like us." And we become guilty of a worse sin than theirs.

the trouble with pride

Whatever the cause, pride's results are devastating. The seed of pride inevitably produces a bad crop. Exposing its final destination may urge us to turn around before it's too late. Here's the trouble with pride.

God hates pride

God hates pride perhaps more than any other sin. He has resolved to expose and punish it. Pride makes him angry. He has promised in his Word to bring low those who elevate themselves. And he will keep his word. If we are intent on pleasing God, we must be cleansed of pride because he will not abide it. This alone should be enough reason to abandon all pride now and in the future.

people will hate us

People love to watch the fall of great people. "The bigger they are, the harder they fall," we gleefully say. Most people secretly revel in the demise of a proud man or woman. But this is not the worst of it. It's waiting for the fall, the yearning for another's collapse that is the greater evil. Pride provides the temptation of others to envy—that unseemly desire to see the downfall of another. The more pride others see in us, the more they will hope for *our* downfalls. Proud people may have power, prestige, money, and influence. But the proud have fewer friends.

pride ignites other sins

It is difficult to commit just one sin. Sin comes in clusters. Pride is especially prone to blend with other sins. At the very least, pride will lead to boasting, being proud out loud. After all, once we are convinced of our greatness, why not tell others? But pride also leads to arrogance, conceit, vanity, and haughtiness. We will eventually become cocky and condescending, totally wrapped up in ourselves. If pride is not eliminated early, it can eventually make hated, egotistical people out of us.

we will undervalue others

Those who overestimate themselves undervalue others. The higher and better we think we are, the lower and lesser we will assume everyone else is. Pride leads us to disdain others. Inevitably, we will come to dismiss both the people's work and the people themselves as insignificant. If we have the power, our scorn for others will result in creating an oppressive atmosphere where we rule as absolute monarch—at work, school, or worst of all, at home. Eventually, we will dismiss others, even loved ones, as idiots, morons, or stooges, wondering to ourselves,

"Why do I have to do *everything*? Can't someone else do things right just once?"

pride produces resentment in others

If we are proud bosses, we'll produce resentment in our employees. If we are not the boss, our pride produces resentment inside ourselves. We'll say that we deserve to be treated better, that we're being used and receive no recognition. We think we are the key and that without us, everything would fall apart.

we will attempt to impress others

Proud people are not satisfied in being their only admirer. Pride drives us to all sorts of attempts to make others think we're great. The prideful will attempt to impress others with indulgent and excessive living. We name-drop to show how important we are. We delight in telling power-stories of how we wielded influence or wealth. We do not recognize how others see through these pitiful attempts to inflate our personal greatness. We think our practices of name-dropping and expensive lifestyles have actually impressed everybody. But the people are not fooled.

pride makes us practical atheists

Perhaps this is why God reserves special wrath for pride. In pride, we discard gratitude to God and assume that we ourselves have accomplished our success. We become our own creators and sustainers of life, becoming guilty of the master sin: self-worship. "Who needs God? We can do it ourselves! We've *already* done it ourselves." Is atheism far behind? Isn't this already a form of atheism? No wonder God urges us to put off pride!

Pride usurps the glory rightfully due God and others. Why do we have wealth? Success? Knowledge? Talent? Creativity? Virtue? Did we get it on our own? Do we think we really are self-made? Do we worship our Creator? Or do we have others to thank? Isn't it true that we have nothing but what came to us by the hand of God and others? Pride will tell us otherwise. Pride lies, and then it utterly destroys.

pride eventually leads to collapse

Pride leads to overconfidence. The more we inflate our self-opinions, the more we become cocky, rash, and confident that we are the exception to the rule. We are above the laws of God and man, or so we act. The more successful we become, the more we risk. Finally, our unrealistic lives break with reality. Life comes crashing down around our ears. We've overextended our sensible limits. This is God's natural law. God has spoken: "Pride goes before destruction, a haughty spirit before a fall" (Prov. 16:18). There is no such thing as permanent pride. It is bound to collapse.

how to begin practicing humility

We have met this monster, pride, and have come to recognize its causes and consequences, but how do we get rid of it? Do *you* have pride? Does this all sound familiar or strange to you?

If you are moving along in your Christian walk and growing in maturity, take some time for self-examination on this point. During times of such quiet thought, we often hear God's voice gently pointing out a sprout of pride. A day alone with God or a morning quiet time may give him the opportunity to speak. Most of us are so busy that a tiny sprout of pride can grow to become a full vine, entwining all our attitudes before we notice. Give God a chance. Take some time to listen. He is faithful and will convict your heart if this is an area for which you should seek his cleansing. If he convicts you of pride, take the prescriptions offered here.

confess and repent

Start by openly admitting your sinful pride before the Lord, then make a decision to turn away from it with full intention to never turn back. This is confession and repentance. There will be no healing until you first admit your need.

spend time with "humblers"

Some people are marvelously gifted at humbling others. I'm not talking about negative-thinking balloon-poppers who delight in putting people down with caustic and sarcastic taunts. Rather, I mean certain people who are clever, fast-thinking, and witty, people who don't take others too seriously. Being with people like this can help you to quit taking yourself so seriously.

If you know such a person, spend some time with him or her. It is hard to be proud around this type of person. His or her remarks will remind you of who you really are. Children are especially good "humblers." Adults don't awe them. They simply know us as Dad, Mom, or Grandpa. Like the little boy who announced that the emperor had no clothes on, they see us for who we really are. If you have no associates who humble you periodically, find some. Take this medicine; it will be good for you.

occasionally compare yourself upwards

Generally, comparison does little good at all. The proud man has gotten into the habit of comparison—downward. He surveys those scattered below him, comparing them to his own great achievements. These underachievers seem so puny from his perspective. He thus sustains his grandiose view of himself. The prescription: simply reverse this habit. Compare yourself *upward*. Are you a superb golfer? Watch the Masters Tournament. Are you wealthy? Compare yourself with some of the *really* wealthy people. Do you think you are the best preacher in your area? Sit under the feeding ministry of a great, old "war horse" preacher and watch your preacher pride wither.

adopt humbling disciplines

If you battle with pride, purposely adopt several disciplines of humility. Return some grocery carts to the store from the parking lot. Stop on your way to the office and spend ten minutes picking up paper on the grass. Change a tire on someone's car. Pick up any trash and straighten the hymnals after church one day. Are these chores beneath you? Try to think of several humbling disciplines you could start doing to continually deflate your pride. Jesus washed his disciples' feet as such a discipline. What could you do?

seek cleansing

Pride is not something outward we can easily drop aside, but there are such things in the Bible. We are simply told to put them off, like old clothing or clinging burrs picked up after a walk in the woods. Pride is different. It resides within, deep within. "Put off" may be an inadequate concept for getting rid of pride. Two other biblical terms may better describe the need: *cleansing* and *crucifixion*.

Anyone who has wrestled with pride knows it is not easily dropped aside like a dirty piece of clothing. It clings to your nature, forming an alloy with the metal of your soul. You who fight it need something radical. You need cleansing—a God-initiated purifying act in your heart. Seek crucifixion, the execution of this evil inclination within. Certainly you must do your part, but only God can complete the work of purification necessary to cleanse you of pride. And he is faithful. He will do it. God catalogs no sin from which his followers cannot be free. God's grace is greater than all your sin, even a taint so deep as pride!

what about you?

Exposing pride is not an easy task. It is neither fun nor entertaining. But pride is a troublesome sin that God would like to remove from your life. And he will do it. Do you have pride? *Any* pride? If so, confess it to our Lord. Seek his forgiveness and cleansing. You can trust him. After all, cleansing is his business.

Of course, you should also be careful not to become obsessed with this sin. Sometimes we assume if all our sins were cast out of our hearts we would be perfect Christians. Wrong. Each of these homeless devils would gather six other devils and return to again occupy the empty houses of our souls. We would be worse off than before. Nature abhors a vacuum; so does God. Perfection is not emptiness.

Rather, you must fill your mind and soul with good things. Virtues are much stronger than vices. For every vice, there is an opposite virtue. For pride, it's humility. Do you hunger for a meek and humble spirit that makes a completely accurate estimate of yourself, neither inflated nor depressed? Do you yearn for the humility that prompts service? Do you always look for opportunities to affirm other people, forever seeking to encourage, praise, and honor others? Do you crave the humble attitude that Jesus had? You can have it. All of this and more are included in God's plan for your life. "God opposes the proud but gives grace to the humble" (1 Pet. 5:5). Are you thirsty enough to drink in great gulps of Christ's humility? Ask God for an avalanche of humility in your life. He can cleanse your pride and fill you with a humble spirit.

What are your specific plans to practice the discipline of humility this week?

19. purifying ambition

Whoever wants to become great among you must be your servant.
—*Matthew 20:26*

Several years ago, a bright, young fellow on his way to success posed a serious question. This guy was a hardworking, promising lad. He always showed up on time, performed his assignments and tasks with excellence, and inevitably put out the extra effort to achieve excellence. I call this type of person a sharpy or producer.

One day, this young man came to me deeply disturbed. He wondered if his motivation was wholly proper. He thought there must be such a thing as good ambition, but he wasn't sure his unquenchable thirst for success was completely pure. In fact, he confessed he suspected it was mostly impure. He sensed he wanted to get ahead simply for the power, prestige, money, and influence it would bring him. "Is this wrong?" was his question.

What would you have said? What's the difference between good ambition and carnal one-upmanship? How can you tell which you have?

There are some people who worry too much about their motivations. These Christians don't get much done in the world because they're always checking themselves for improper motivations. Like hypochondriacs, they constantly invent spiritual illnesses. This is the Devil's trick to keep such tender Christians preoccupied with themselves instead of a needy world. I'm not addressing these remarks to such people. (If you have such an extraordinary sensitivity, this might even be a chapter to skip.) But if you seldom worry about your motivations and are a hard-driving, success-oriented person, the Lord may direct some words specifically to you in this chapter.

motivation and ambition

Right intentions can purify deeds. The New Testament repeatedly reminds us that we can be judged "blameless" by God if our intentions are pure, even though the actual result falls pitifully below the absolute standard of perfection. Because of ignorance or spiritual immaturity, we may offer up a "spotted sacrifice" to God in our words, thoughts, or deeds. Yet if our intentions were pure—completely out of hunger to please God—he pronounces us blameless in his sight. God holds us accountable for what we say, think, or do *purposefully*.

In this God does nothing more than we would do. For instance, last year my house was in desperate need of painting. Due to a pressing travel and speaking schedule, I decided to hire a painter to do the job. After mentioning it one night at the dinner table, my twelve-year-old son piped up, "Hey, Dad, I'll paint the house. I could really use the money." What was I to do? I took the risk and gave him the job. He recruited another twelve-year-old to help him and plunged into the work with a hearty vigor (which began to wane during the hot days of August)! After several weeks, he finished the job and was ready for my final inspection and his payday. He had worked harder than I had ever seen him work before. I could see that he had taken special care to avoid spilling drops of paint and splotching the trim paint on the siding. He had carefully scraped and peeled away large slabs of the old paint before adding the fresh coat. In some places, he had carefully applied two coats to ensure complete coverage.

As we slowly examined our way around the house, I noticed an occasional slip-up, a smudge of blue trim on the siding or a few drops of yellow paint on the shrubs. As we completed the final inspection, I remembered that he had never painted anything before in his life. I was justifiably proud of his hard work. As we finished the walk around, he turned and gazed expectantly into my face. "How'd I do, Dad?" he asked.

What do you think I said? I responded, "David, you've done a *perfect* job!" and gave him a great bear hug in appreciation. I paid him and even gave him a bonus.

Would God do less? No. He considers our experiences, the difficulties of our assignments, our maturity, and the motivations of our hearts. Like a loving father, he sometimes pronounces our work perfect even when he can see a smudge here and there. Only God has the wisdom to pronounce us blameless. Only he knows our true motivations. When our motivations are pure, God pronounces our deeds pure.

Conversely, pure deeds can be polluted by foul motivations. Jesus reserved his most scathing condemnation for the Pharisees. They loved to engage in holy activities, especially praying and giving, but did these things out of impure motivation, to be seen or considered holy by other people. Impure motivations can defile the best of deeds.

So what does all this have to do with ambition? Ambition itself is not wrong. Sin enters the picture at the motivation level. Why are we ambitious? It is our motivations for getting ahead and the methods we use that determine the sinfulness of ambition. Consider three levels of ambition.

holy ambition

Some ambition is outright holy. Holy ambition is a pure, pointed mandate from God. It is a call to complete a task or mission. It is closely connected with the ideas of a call or destiny. Having holy ambition is to know for sure that God is calling us to do something. We believe we have come to the kingdom for such a time as this. It is hungering for obedience to our Master more than for mere accomplishment and success. Holy ambition produces a calm, unruffled drive like that of Jesus Christ, who never seemed to be in a hurry yet always knew where he was headed. Holy ambition is the conviction that God has called us to do something, and nothing in or under the world can stop us. It is a holy compulsion driving us to achievement as a matter of obedience, not as a matter of personal success.

Holy ambition drives us to succeed because we believe this is God's will for us—not a general kind of will, in the sense that God expects all of us to do a good job, but in a personal way. It is a compulsion from God. We feel that God has called us personally to achieve this thing. We believe that God intends to accomplish this special work through us. It is his will, not ours. We are certain that this is God's will for our lives, and we feel destined to achieve it.

Holy ambition is not common.

human aspiration

This kind of ambition is neither good nor bad; it is simply human. God has created us with a longing for achievement, fulfillment, even greatness. We have a hunger for significance, a desire for something better, something lasting. All of us have this yearning, Christian or not. The innate desire to achieve, create, and improve, is stamped on our nature by the Creator. It is a glimpse of one way we are created in his image. It is a drive to do better, accomplish something, and leave something worthwhile behind.

These human aspirations are not sin; they are wholesome. This desire for excellence, accomplishment, and betterment comes from God. Most progress in civilization springs from this God-given drive. Christians, of all people, should fan these human embers of achievement into flame, for he is "able to do immeasurably more than all we ask or imagine, according to his power that is at work within us" (Eph. 3:20). Most of us are achieving far below our potential. If we fear success, somehow thinking that failure is holy or honorable, we are wrong. Jesus clearly taught that the man who buries his potential in the ground will receive strict rejection from his master (see Matt. 25:14–30).

God expects us to invest and multiply the talents and opportunities he has given us, because he is the one who has given us the desires of human aspiration. These are neither good nor bad; what they lead to will determine their goodness or badness.

selfish ambition

Here is the lowest level of ambition. Selfish ambition crosses the line from human aspiration into selfishness because the motivation is impure. Selfish ambition is sin. It springs from the flesh. It is the desire to be lord over others, to possess the power of success. It is the desire to beat others, be number one, and win for winning's sake. It is healthy competition turned into hellish combativeness. Selfish ambition is a hunger for power, prestige, and status. It thirsts for recognition, rewards, and the influence that comes with success. This kind of ambition propels us to trample competitors and climb over friends to achieve success. With selfish ambition, once we make it to the next highest level, we quickly kick down old friends who helped us get there. They are no longer useful in climbing to the next step of greatness. It is this kind of ambition that is sin and out of place in the Christian's life.

mixed motivation

For most of us, our aspirations cannot be neatly divided between the three levels. Sometimes there is mixed motivation in our desire for achievement. While we may not claim that our ambition is of the holy type, we usually feel it is of the wholesome, human variety—at least, mostly so. Mostly? Herein lies the problem of selfish ambition. Who would say that their ambition is wholly selfish? Few. Such people are not Christian at all, but believers may come to recognize that this ambition is partly selfish. Satan does not attempt to turn wholesome ambition into evil in a day or even a year. Rather, he injects the poison of selfish ambition one drop at a time. Each tiny additional drop seems minute compared with the whole. We may not even recognize this poisoning process at first. Even when we recognize it, we dismiss this part of our motivation as inconsequential. Then we comfort ourselves with the thought that our motivations are mostly pure. But these tiny drops of selfish ambition multiply and taint our entire motivation. The Devil, once given a foothold, is intent on expanding his territory. Like yeast, selfish ambition soon spreads its influence throughout the whole dough of our hearts.

No serious Christian can be satisfied with ambition that is mostly pure. The part of our ambition that is selfish must be cleansed, or it will stain the whole.

degenerating ambition

Ambition has a tendency to start out right then get off track. Human aspiration can be 100 percent wholesome at first yet later derail into selfish ambition. We can start out with a clean, God-given desire to succeed, yet as time passes, selfish ambition leaks into our motivations, and we become selfish. We must constantly be on guard against the Devil's attempts to introduce microscopic molecules of selfish ambition into our motivations. We must be constantly aware of these attempts to subvert our wholesome human motivations. It is clear that human aspiration can degenerate into selfish ambition.

being power hungry

Even more serious is the degeneration of holy ambition into selfish ambition. God may call some people to a great task. At first, the people's motivation is completely holy. They are obsessed with following God and God alone. However, as they find success, Satan begins to introduce the twin sisters of success: pride and selfish ambition. Soon the spiritual giant allows selfish ambition to make its bed beside the original holy ambition. The two lie together, and the people become tainted by selfish ambition.

This is the danger of seeking a powerful anointing from God.

People who seek God's outward power but do not have his inward purity are destined to collapse. Their great ministries are houses of cards; the higher they go, the greater they fall. When God answers their prayers for power, they are increasingly used in the kingdom. They plunge onward and upward, constructing ever-expanding ministries teetering on foundations of sand. Finally, their personal towers of Babel reach God's predetermined limit. It all comes crashing down in moral collapse. They exit in ridicule and humiliation. The rest of us scurry about, covering up the mess to preserve God's reputation and the church's good name. It doesn't work. The truth gets out. Everyone eventually discovers that these "great leaders" were hollow heroes. The outer shells were magnificent, but the inner moral timbers were infested with termites.

Yet God is glorified. How? Following the people's downfall, the church lays aside its secular preoccupation with outward power and talks in hushed tones about the importance of inward purity for a time.

Do you hunger for more power from God? Have you been selfishly seeking God's outer anointing on your life? Beware. Just as he answered Israel's prayer for a king, God may answer your prayer. But if you do not have his inner purity, you too will collapse. It is clear, isn't it? Even our quest in spiritual matters may become tainted with selfish ambition. Like Simon Magus, we can hunger for God's power with selfish motivation (see Acts 8:18–21).

how to recognize selfish ambition

But how are we to know if our ambitions are selfish? Is there some test we can take? Is there some wise sage we can visit who can tell us for sure? It's not that easy; however, with some reflection, the Holy Spirit is always reliable to point out sin in our lives. This is his work; give him a chance to speak, and you can be sure that if you have any selfish ambitions, he will expose them. Ponder the following questions as you listen to the Spirit. Is he saying anything to you? Say something like Samuel did: "Speak, for your servant is listening" (1 Sam. 3:10). If you hear nothing, then joyfully move on to the next chapter with a clear heart. But if he speaks, seek his cleansing of your ambitions. Ponder these questions. Perhaps grade yourself in each of these areas:

- Am I more interested in the glory than the goal?
- How do I feel when someone else starts to accomplish "my thing" or fulfills my dream? Do I rejoice or have a tinge of jealousy?
- Am I preoccupied with the means more than the goal?
- Do I visualize myself doing or being the dream, or do I visualize the recipients receiving the benefit of my work?
- Am I obsessed with power, money, prestige, or influence?

- Is my ambition short-term, or has it been long lasting in my life? Has it marinated for several years, or is it really merely a temporary brainstorm?
- Is it specific and definable or unspecific and hard to explain?
- Is it need-oriented, growing out of a burden to serve people, or does it grow out of my desire for achievement?
- Do those in spiritual and administrative authority over me give confirmation of this ambition? Do they say, "Go for it," or are they giving caution signals?
- Do those around me volunteer to help me accomplish this great ambition?
- Am I obsessed with the accomplishment of this goal?
- Am I willing to pay the price to see it happen, or do I want someone to hand it to me on a silver platter?
- Can I visualize the results?
- Do my spouse, parents, and Christian friends confirm this ambition?
- Would I feel released if God raised up somebody else who did it better than me?
- Have I dropped friends and associates who helped get me where I am?
- In what way would God get glory if I achieved my deepest ambition?
- Have I compromised any of my personal standards to get where I am now?

how to begin purifying ambition

Do you sense that part of your ambition is stained with self-ishness? What are you to do? Is there a means of purifying your human ambition? How will you keep it pure?

This is not one of those areas where you seek a single cleansing then forget the problem forever. True, you may need a crisis cleansing of your selfish ambition; you may need to die to your dreams; you may need to offer your dreams on the altar. But dead ambition may rise again to haunt you. The Devil doesn't give up that easily.

However, you need not feel that you are plagued with this sin forevermore. Selfish ambition can be crucified. If you take the antidote, the poison of selfish ambition can be neutralized in your soul.

reflection

Take some time for introspection. Not the morbid kind of self-abuse that some do, but a positive time of silence and listening before the Lord. Give him a chance to speak. He is not an angry, brutish God, seeking to crush you under the load of your weaknesses and sin. Rather, he is a loving Shepherd seeking to gently nudge you onto the path of righteousness. Take some time for him to nudge you. Don't put this book down without taking a few minutes to listen to what he has to say to you. Read over the questions listed earlier. Ask yourself if any part of your ambition is selfish.

call it by name

If you sense the Lord pointing out selfishness in your desire to achieve, call it by name: selfish ambition, and sin. Until you concede a particular attitude is sin, you will seldom see it purified. Once you call it by name, victory and cleansing can come. Be honest; name it.

confess to another

It may not be absolutely necessary, but you will make great strides toward victory if you share your inclination to selfish ambition with a friend. This humbling act will give you a powerful jump-start toward banishing selfish impurity from your ambition. This person may even agree to hold you accountable, checking in with you from time to time on the extent of your progress in casting out selfish ambition. If you were to do this, with whom could you share such a thing? Is there someone you could trust enough to confess this selfishness to?

die out

It's an old-fashioned term, but worthy of reconsideration today. *Die out* means surrendering personal hopes, aspirations, and dreams on God's altar of commitment. It is sacrificing your personal ambitions on the altar of consecration, like Abraham offered up Isaac. Dying out is surrendering your most-precious desires for achievement to the Lord, assuming you will never get them back. (You may, but if you assume so, the sacrifice is not totally surrendered.)

Dying sometimes takes time. Though there is such a thing as sudden death, more often death is a slow (and painful) process. You may enter a period of dying out. Selfish ambition dies slowly. It tenaciously clings to life. This sin may die at once or gradually, but you can start the process of execution.

recognize that God's focus is inward

Our secular mind-set overtakes us. We assume God, like us, is more concerned with what he does through us than what he does in us. In this we err. If God has a preoccupation, it is with your inside—attitudes, thoughts, motivations, and personal purity. Inside quality lasts; outside quantity fades. When you realize God is more concerned with your inner attitudes than your outward success, you will be able to lay aside your secular fixation with climbing the ladder.

focus on Christ as your example

Are you ambitious? Then think of Christ. How would you measure his success? Was Jesus a winner? Would you consider Jesus Christ a high achiever? Was he a ladder climber? How high did he climb? Did he make it to the top? He did! The height of his career was played out at the top of Calvary's hill. Like us, his disciples wondered who would have the place of precedence—to his right and left—when he came into his kingdom (see Matt. 20:21).When Jesus hung on Calvary's hill, to the right and left hung unknown thieves on cruel crosses.

Jesus had it all: he was (and is) God's Son; he was (and is) God. Yet he humbled himself to become a man, a common carpenter. He chose to be obedient to God. This was success for him: obedience, even unto death—painful death on a cross. And what did the Father do? God then exalted Jesus to the highest place of all. Didn't the Father give him a name that will ultimately send every knee bowing? Isn't this how the Father responds to humble servanthood?

In your obsession with your own success, you may lose sight of Jesus Christ. You overdose on success formula talks by others who have "made it." Each person has his or her own ten steps to success for you. Some flaunt their wealth, influence, and power as evidence of their success, and you are impressed. You, too, begin to hunger for worldly wealth, fame, and power. And selfish ambition is born.

Instead, look to Jesus. Seek the attitude he had, being willing to give it all up in order to obey the Father. Jesus' example inspires true success—obedience.

seek cleansing

Some sins you can lay aside with God's help. Others you can seemingly drop yourself. A few sins, however, require radical surgery from God. Selfish ambition will not be beaten by a simple three-step prescription. God's grace is great enough to forgive you of this sin, but his grace is even greater than that. He will cleanse you of this inclination. God's grace seeks nothing less than the total transformation of your entire life into Christlikeness. If you have selfish ambition, you must do something about it. But you need not rid yourself of this taint by yourself. God is able to grant you transforming power to correct this fleshly attitude. His grace is great enough to cleanse this selfishness of the spirit, purifying your ambition. This is the kind of God you serve!

what about you?

Has God pricked your own soul about your ambition? Do not listen to the voices around you; listen to God alone. What does he say? Do you have selfish ambition? Is your ambition partly selfish? If so, seek God's cleansing. Seek the death of this yeast before it spreads its evil leaven into the whole loaf of your life. God will do it. He is in the transforming business. Ask him and see!

What are your specific plans to practice the discipline of purifying ambition this week?

20. honesty

*Therefore each of you must put off falsehood and speak truthfully
to his neighbor, for we are all members of one body.*

—Ephesians 4:25

Do you remember your first lie? I was about five or six years
old when I told my first lie. An older boy from down the street
led me off on a great exploration of the woods behind the park a
few blocks from my house. My parents had forbidden me to go
beyond a two-block limit, but Columbus and Magellan beckoned.
Off I went, exploring uncharted territories. When I returned
home, my mother asked where I'd been. I lied.

Lying is pervasive in our society. We have come to admit
and accept lying as necessary in our world today. Governments
lie as a matter of routine. As a teenager in 1960, I was
wounded to discover that "Honest Ike" had lied to the world
about Francis Gary Powers's U2 flight over Russia. My old
war hero confessed to the world that he had lied, even

defended it as "necessary" to protect his country's interests. I was disappointed.

Then came President Nixon who told some whoppers in his self-righteous sort of way. He came tumbling down through the efforts of two reporters from *The Washington Post* who told a number of lies of their own as they tracked down the president's lies. Jody Powell occasionally admitted he lied about Carter's policies. And in the Iran-Contra scandal during the Reagan administration, lies were elevated by some to be judged heroic and quite necessary. Then came Bill Clinton and the following decades of deceivers in both their public and private lives.

Of course, lying is not new. America's practice of breaking treaties with Native Americans is a shameful blot on its past. The truth is, we are a society of liars. We've even come to take lying lightheartedly. Many years ago, David Leisure climbed to fabulous fame and wealth by age thirty-seven in Isuzu Motors' twenty-million-dollar TV "Liar Campaign." Joe Isuzu enthusiastically made preposterous verbal claims for the Isuzu cars while captions underneath him read, "He's lying."

I can remember taking my car to a church member to get a quote on some body work. Worried about the expense, I asked, "How much is this going to cost me?" His reply: "You gonna pay cash or do you need a receipt?" I needed a receipt and said so. His reply: "That'll cost you more; got to pay Uncle Sam, ya know." Do Christians sometimes lie?

The world's sinking standard of truth often creeps into the church body until we adopt the world's standards. Even ministers get caught in the web of truth-stretching and exaggeration. Is your church letting down the standard of absolute honesty? Are you hiding, stretching, or shading the truth?

kinds of lying

Most Christians would condemn a bold-faced lie. We are not likely to get caught telling such outright falsehoods. But there are other forms of lying that sometimes trip up believers. Christians are more likely to be tempted to deliver *half-truths*, partially true statements (that are also partially false). Or there is *flattery*, insincere praise. There are *false excuses*, not giving the real reason for one's actions. There are *false impressions*, using words that are technically true but designed to give the hearer a totally different idea. Christians may be tempted to *exaggeration*, stretching facts and stories for effect. There is *deceit*, contriving a false reputation for oneself. Sometimes believers may be tempted to *suppress the truth*, keeping silent when the truth is needed. I would hope no Christian would be guilty of *slander*, spreading false stories told with the intention to harm. But believers might be caught in *white lies*, falsehoods told for a good cause. The Devil is the Father of Lies and has been exceedingly creative in providing a varied choice of methods for the person who wishes to be less than absolutely honest.

This chapter will not deal with every kind of lying. This chapter intends to focus on only three areas where church people, even ministers, are tempted to lie.

lying about numbers

How we love to stretch numbers! The church-growth movement has spawned some fine growth and success in churches. In the quest for success and local church fame, we try to grow and increase. If we can't, we sometimes take the easy shortcut to success—lying about numbers. Back in the days when church bus programs were at their height, I heard of one pastor who couldn't get the bus attendance up to his predecessor's. He called across the country to find out his predecessor's secret. The answer: "Oh, I always added fifty to the total . . . you know, for the ones I might have missed." Another pastor once told me he examined the actual local records of his predecessor and compared them with what was reported to the district. He discovered as much as a 50 percent variance from week to week. A third young pastor wrote a heartbreaking letter, reporting the sad story of how his predecessor had simply looked over the crowd each Sunday and said, "Looks like a good Sunday. I'd say we have about 350 here today." No actual counting was done. The estimated attendance was reported for years to church officials. The young new pastor had carefully counted people one by one. The records showed a precipitous drop of as many as a hundred people, yet the attendees said that the crowds seemed about the same or larger. He wrote, "I'm afraid people are going to say 'that young fellow went in there and simply ruined that church.'"

The standard question church people—especially ministers—ask each other is, "How many do you have?" The pressure for a successful answer is high. Has your church become loose with the truth? I know of one pastor's exaggeration that had become such a laughing matter to his congregation that they secretly dubbed him Pastor Pinocchio.

But it is not just ministers under success pressure who sometimes lie. Church members are equally as bad. Sometimes the members inflate current numbers, but more often they magnify past numbers. One pastor was continually hounded by a fellow who frequently greeted him at the door with something like, "Well, preacher, you had one hundred fifty today, but back when Reverend Otis was here, we ran over two hundred every single Sunday. Yep, those were great days." This pastor was so annoyed by the constant irritation that he drove to his district headquarters to peruse the record books. The records showed that the church had never averaged over two hundred for even one month, though they did have several big days when the attendance exceeded two hundred. Like yeast, the attendance had grown as the old fellow had let it rise in his mind over time.

Some Christians jokingly call this kind of numerical exaggeration "evangelistically speaking." Have we become so dulled to honesty that we brazenly attach the sacred concept of "evangelistic" to this kind of truth-stretching? It is an awful abuse of the word *evangelistic*. God prefers the more accurate term: *lying*. Lying is not evangelistic; it is devilish.

lying about accomplishments

This, too, is a snare for church people: lying about what we've done in the past. Local church leaders are simply overwhelmed to discover that in a prospective candidate's last church, there were only twenty-six in the first service, and just last month he had 286. Wow! "Let's get this fellow here. Maybe he can do that sort of thing for us," they say.

What the leaders weren't told is that the fellow's first service was a midweek prayer meeting in August! "Just last month" the 286 attendance was on Easter Sunday. They somehow got the impression that the *average* attendance had risen from twenty-six to 286. False impressions if made intentionally are lies.

Ministers in search of a new church often hide half-truths about accomplishments in their résumés. Sure, résumés are supposed to present people's abilities and accomplishments in the best possible light. But in the quest for honor, it's easy to puff up our accomplishments until they become outright lies.

Local church leaders are no better. When a new candidate is interviewed, the leaders frequently paint a much rosier picture of the church and its people than is true. A pastor recently told me at lunch, "The church purely and simply lied to me." Sure, you don't have to tell a candidate everything. But purposefully masking a church's problems and willfully painting a rosier picture than is true is clearly lying.

I have heard at least a dozen ministers say something like, "I had no idea what I was getting myself into. Everything was painted rosy to me." And a few members have said after a messy situation developed with their pastor, "We had no idea he had this problem, and we find out this happened twice before at other churches. *Now* they tell us!"

Lies about our accomplishments can eventually become such a part of our own psyches that we can come to believe them ourselves. Total reality breakdown is then not far behind. Why do we inflate our accomplishments? We think we have to impress people. We're afraid that the bare truth just isn't outstanding, interesting, or comical enough. So we embellish our past in an attempt to impress and entertain others. But others *know* it!

The lie detector provides more evidence of what Christians have known all along—we can tell when someone is lying.

Sure, there are hidden physical signs: increased heartbeat, perspiration, and imperceptible changes in breathing measured by the polygraph. But there are visible open signs too: voice tone, eye movement, and body language. These outward signs are picked up by listeners. The listener's subconscious mind collects and processes all this data and feeds a mental impression to the listener's mind: "He's lying!" People carry their own lie detectors around with them. When someone is inflating their accomplishments, others can sense it. Perhaps they can't prove it, but for some reason or another, they don't feel they can trust this story. It is their own inner polygraph telling them not to trust the person speaking.

lying in stories and illustrations

I know the acceptable speaker's routine. Dig around a bit to get ideas. Listen to a couple of CDs and read a few books. Then a teacher or speaker makes it his or her own by developing illustrations similar to the ones read or heard.

This is a realistic plan, but it is full of danger: counterfeit illustrations. Face it—some of our lives just aren't that interesting, or at least we don't see the illustrations in everyday life like others do. The temptation is to make up a similar story based on fact, taking a true experience and embellishing it a bit. Invent a few additional lines of narrative. Embellish the story by tossing in a few extra "facts" and soon we have a great illustration. After all, it keeps the listeners awake. It's all for a good cause, isn't it?

Many years ago, I had the opportunity to travel from camp to camp during one summer. One particular preacher had an itinerary that crisscrossed mine. The first time I heard his message on evangelism, it was glorious. He told how he had witnessed to a fellow on the plane on the way to the camp the day before. The fellow hadn't made a decision, but the preacher could tell he was under conviction. He even had given the preacher his address and promised to start attending church. I was impressed with this message on evangelism. So were the people. Here was a speaker who really practiced what he preached. He was calling us to witness, and he had done it the day before on the plane!

At a later camp, I ran into this speaker again, and he told the story again. This time he added the line that big tears were running down the man's cheeks. Perhaps he'd forgotten that detail in the first telling? People loved it! There was a big altar response — people wanting to share their faith like this man.

By the end of the summer, the tale had grown so tall that the speaker had the man on the plane receiving Christ with several people around them crying, as the onlookers also expressed interest in receiving Christ. "We had a prayer meeting right there on that plane," he tearfully said as he closed his sermon. The people fervently applauded. The only trouble is the story was a lie. I wondered if the first story was even true. This man was practicing preacher perjury. We all would condemn this kind of pastoral lying. Wouldn't we?

Do you lie? What about those little white lies? Do you decorate your stories? How about that hunting tale of that twelve-point buck? Do you lie about your age? When was the last time you listed or told someone your weight? Was it true? Do you tell stories of your military days? College days? Are they true? Are you a fisherman? What about that four-mile walk you took to school each day as a child. Was it *really* four miles uphill both ways in the snow (all year round)? Are these innocent exaggerations? God doesn't think so. God figures his children should tell the simple, unadulterated truth. Forked tongues belong in the Serpent's family, not God's.

The church—especially we who are speakers—should renew our commitment to honesty in stories and illustrations. Let's make a fresh start at truthful storytelling, even if our friends or audiences go to sleep.

how to begin practicing honesty

mean what you say

The church needs a renewed commitment to absolute honesty in numbers. Our yes should be yes and our no, no (see Matt. 5:37). And our two hundred should be two hundred, not 190.

tell the whole truth

Do you lie about your accomplishments? It is time for Christians to start telling the truth, the whole truth, and nothing but the truth so help us God—even on résumés. The church should be a place where we accept and affirm each other as people of worth. Would you rather have a successful liar for a pastor or a mediocre honest person?

speak in love

As Christians we must put off all manner of lying and start to speak the absolute truth to each other, speaking "the truth in love" (Eph. 4:15). There is nothing loving about lying.

listen to your spouse

If you are married, be sure to listen to your spouse. After one great ministerial liar was exposed, I always wondered, "Where was his wife?" She traveled with him often and certainly knew he was lying. Didn't she call him on it? Perhaps she thought, "God's using him, so I'd better keep quiet." Or maybe she spoke up and he refused to listen. I don't know. But I do know my wife monitors my speaking (and writing) carefully. If I stretch a fact or story, she confronts me. If your husband or wife corrects a figure or a story, take it like a Christian. It might keep you from becoming an even bigger liar.

what about you?

What are your specific plans to practice the discipline of honesty this week?

21. peacemaking

Peacemakers who sow in peace raise a harvest of righteousness.
—James 3:18

Peacemakers are supposed to be blessed, according to the Sermon on the Mount. But what is a peacemaker? How are we to make peace or sow peace? Where are we to do it? Why are we to do it?

Peacemaking is an uncommon discipline of holy living. Though the prescription for healing division is common sense, obeying God's recommendations for peacemaking is where we have trouble.

how division develops

No two snowflakes and no two people are alike. God is a God of orderliness but not of uniformity. His creation is one of infinite variety. His crowning creation, man, is especially varied. Humanity represents a broad spectrum of assorted fascinating personalities, temperaments, and racial and ethnic traits.

Some of us are shy and passive, while others are outgoing and aggressive. Some are sensitive and emotional, while others are logical, never letting their feelings show. Some of us are orderly, organized, and perfectionists. The rest of us are messy, disorganized, and forgetful.

differences cause interpersonal friction

Friction occurs in interpersonal relationships when we spend time with people different from ourselves. The shy, quiet person is irritated by the outgoing, boisterous person. The orderly person thinks the disorganized person is a slob. Energetic hard-drivers think easygoing people are lazy wimps. The easygoing person returns the assessment, considering the hard-driver a fascist dictator who runs roughshod over everyone who gets in his or her way.

When interpersonal friction occurs, we tend to see another's personality strength as a weakness. The neat are considered fastidious. Bold people are considered brash. Sensitive people are termed touchy. The humorous become silly; the cautious are fearful; and the frugal become tightwads. The strengths of others become the very targets of our criticism. Nowhere is this seen so clearly as in marriage. Differences cause friction.

We have mentioned only personality traits thus far. What about differing opinions on politics, theology, worship music, or religious convictions? What about differing personal preferences, like when someone should go to bed or what someone should eat (or not eat) for breakfast or which way should the toilet paper hang on the dispenser? The possibilities for interpersonal friction are immeasurable, but it is to be expected. We are to treat these irritations with grace and acceptance. Friction is not sin. The next step is the fatal one.

friction can cause broken relationships

Constant friction can lead to relational breakdown. If we do not learn to deal with friction appropriately, it will slowly drive a wedge between relationships so that we eventually break fellowship with one another. We start to avoid each other. We begin leaving by separate doors and avoid mutual friends. Eventually, we each gather several sympathetic friends and factions form. People take sides in our battle. Ultimately, the whole group may be destroyed, simply because the initial broken relationship between two good people wasn't faced and repaired. Have you ever witnessed the battlefield of such a broken relationship? Have you ever seen a whole church eventually destroyed because two or more of God's people didn't make peace?

How can we avoid this senseless slaughter? A quarrel, like a fire, can be quenched early with a pint of water. Left alone it will rage out of control, eventually consuming everything in its path.

how to begin practicing peacemaking

There are four different situations when relational breakdown is possible. Each has its own prescription.

when someone has wronged you

What do you do when you have a grievance against another Christian? Maybe he or she said something harsh and cut you deeply. Perhaps he or she pulled a procedural "end run" play in a committee meeting, and you were omitted from an important assignment you really wanted. What should you do when the pastor pulls a fast one and works you out of the job you've held for seventeen years in your church? How should you respond when someone tells you one of your "friends" told a bit of gossip about you that morning? What are Christians supposed to do when they feel they've been wronged?

Arrange for a Private Talk. Take action—immediately. Don't brood and churn about it any longer. Feeling you've been treated unjustly is the breeding ground for bitterness, a cancer of the soul. This malignancy will grow and spread its tentacles rapidly. So don't wait. Take action. Go and see the one you feel has offended you face-to-face. In such a private encounter, the offender is more likely to confess and restore the relationship. Once others are involved, the stakes are raised and confession is slower to come. Go directly to the person. Don't write a note because it can easily be misconstrued or misunderstood. Go alone and try to straighten this out just between the two of you.

Of course, you must be careful in approaching the individual. Don't be accusatory. Obviously, you shouldn't say, "I heard you told a lie about me, and I've come to see if you did." Merely share why you feel hurt, offering them an opportunity to minister to your hurt. Never go in anger. Calm down first. But don't wait more than a day either. Going in anger may be better than not going at all. Make sure you approach with tenderness. After all, you are attempting to extract a splinter from your brother's eye. Such an operation requires considerable adeptness.

Take a Few Others and Try Again. If you didn't settle the issue between the two of you the first time, take one or two others and go again. Pick a few Christians who are wise, gracious, and highly respected. Obviously, you should not get a hand-picked flock of your own friends who will automatically side with you. Choose impartial, discerning, spiritually minded Christians. Let these mature mediators lead the discussion. Place yourself under their leadership and listen to their counsel and correctives.

This introduction of several impartial, mature believers often completely changes the atmosphere. The two of you in conflict will more easily work it out under their leadership, repairing your relationship. Well, maybe not in every case.

Take It to the Church. If your first two attempts have failed to produce a repaired relationship, take the situation to the church's leadership to whom both of you are accountable. Commit yourselves to live by the decision of the leaders on the matter. If you and your brother or sister are not involved in the same church, then agree together on a panel of people to decide the issue between you. If you can't even agree on this, select one mature leader each, then let these two select the third. The point is that when two Christians are deadlocked, the church leaders should decide the outcome of the dispute.

Forget It! If all the steps above don't bring about peace, simply and quickly dismiss the whole affair. Don't be bitter; get better! Don't brood over the person's refusal to give in. Give up on trying to recover your loss or gain a just settlement. Simply forget it. If he or she is a nonbeliever at heart, treat him or her like any other nonbeliever—hope and pray for his or her salvation. Simply dismiss the whole affair. When the first three steps have failed, forget the whole thing, and get on with your life.

To most of us, this elaborate system seems unnecessary. We'd rather quickly settle disputes, or we don't even try to repair broken relationships. It seems easier to simply break the relationship than to follow this process. After all, you're too busy for all this. "I don't need him (or her) anyway," you may say. But you're wrong. This intricate process is designed because God values interpersonal relationships, especially marriage. It is because a broken relationship is so serious to God that he expects us to go to these seemingly extensive ends to repair the fractured relationship.

So if you feel someone has cheated you, hurt you, or been unfair to you, set up a meeting between the two of you and see if you can clear it up. Start this process to bring about peace. Having a peaceful relationship is worth the effort.

when you have wronged someone

Have you ever sensed that someone was holding something against you? You just knew that a particular person had bad feelings toward you. Perhaps you didn't even know why, but you knew it just the same. When Christians feel this way, what are we to do? Perhaps you discovered another's bad feelings toward you through a third party.

Several years ago, a good friend approached me and told me how one particular fellow was absolutely furious with me. He was angered by what I had said on a certain committee. He knew how I eventually voted and was steamed. My friend encouraged me to go and see this fellow while his anger was still hot. It didn't seem wise to me at first. "Let him cool down," I thought to myself, "then I'll go." But I knew better. It is better to deal with hot anger than smoldering bitterness. So I went. I opened the conversation with, "I've come to see you because I think I've offended you. We may not be able to agree about what I said or how I voted, but we can't have a broken relationship over this or anything else. So I've come to see what I can do to clear the air between us. I love you as a brother and want to keep our relationship right. Can we talk about it?"

In this case, the man was easily entreated, and we spent several hours talking. We traced our relationship and discovered several tender bruises we had given each other in the past. He shared an unrelated personal crisis he was going through, which I knew nothing about. We repeatedly tried to come to agreement on the particular issue but never did. We still disagree, but we understand each other better. Most importantly, we have restored our relationship. Our time ended with a tearful hug, and we continue to consider each other with high esteem to this day.

I learned an important lesson that day. It is hard—perhaps impossible—to come to agreement with everybody. But it *is* possible to keep the relationship going in most cases. The advice is simple: If you sense someone has something against you, go to that person and try to work it out. Go even if you think you are right or you know that person is being immature and petty. Go if the incident was purposeful or accidental, actual or supposed. Take action. Go clear the air between the two of you.

It's fascinating how God works the ends against the middle on these kinds of things. If someone has hurt me, I'm to go to him or her. And he or she is to come to me. Both of us are instructed to fix the relationship. If either one obeys, the relationship can be repaired. This is how important our relationships are to God.

Whether you received the hurt or were the one who did the hurting, you are supposed to go to the other and fix the relationship.

Sometimes neither follows this advice. Occasionally, two believers end up at odds with each other, and neither attempts to go to the other one. What should we do when two other Christians are fighting and self-righteously refusing to bury the hatchet?

when others are quarreling

Suppose several people in your church are fussing, and you are not even involved. Mind your own business, right? That's the conventional wisdom. You tell your children to keep their noses out of other people's business and you follow this advice yourself. When others get into a church scrap, you stand by as a sanctimonious spectator. "Leave them alone," you smugly think. "They'll settle it between themselves." And if either of them followed the peacemaking plans above, they would. But they don't. So you stand by as the flames of fractured relationships blaze hotter and consume marriages, friendships, even entire churches. You say, "Let's remember them in prayer."

There's a pattern to all advice on broken relationships: Get involved. Broken relationships, like broken bones, don't go away if you give them time. Churches that have not settled past broken relationships are now permanently crippled in their ministries. Broken bones often need setting for them to heal. Broken relationships need setting too.

When two or more people in a Christian community are on the outs, the rest of us are to pitch in to fix it. We are the body of Christ, each a particular part. Can the hand say, "Who cares if the heart and lungs break fellowship? Let them settle it themselves.

It's not our business"? If the vital organs of a body cease to function in concert, soon the hand too will be blue, cold, and dead.

Any break in relationship in the body *is* your business! All believers are to work at fixing the fracture. That is not to say that we are to descend on the pair of quarreling people like a cloud of locusts. Common sense and good judgment are in order. The pastor of the church often coordinates this kind of thing. The most mature Christians, the most spiritually minded, will be the ones called for the delicate task of repairing broken relationships.

Why do we often ignore this sensible advice? Why does the church sit sweetly singing every Sunday when we know there are two believers among us with an unseen war raging between them? Why do we stand idly by as homes are being ripped apart by broken relationships? Why don't we make an effort to restore these breaking relationships? Because we are scared. We don't want to get dirty. We don't want to take sides. So we do nothing. Thus, we sadly watch friendships, marriages, even entire churches go swirling down the drain because of fractured relationships. Rescuing the perishing should begin at home!

God has a better plan: Get involved. When relationships start unraveling, the church is supposed to help these believers make peace. We are to get them back together again. This is peacemaking. It is getting involved, taking the time, and helping to repair that relationship about to go through the shredder. It is getting your hands dirty and your ego battered in even the messiest of messes.

And when you do get involved, you mustn't take sides. And don't always hope for a quick fix; these things take time. Gently and tenderly set the bone of this fracture, and then give it time to heal. This is what Christ expects of you. Even if you fail at the whole attempt, and even if you fumble and things turn worse, he wants you to lovingly, carefully, and compassionately get involved when others are quarreling.

If you don't follow this advice, your whole church will become divided into factions. Then the problem will require an even more drastic measure to correct.

when the whole church is divided

Men and women are social creatures. We automatically draw others into the net of our actions and attitudes. What starts out as a simple difference produces friction. This friction eventually can produce a fracture in relationships. Now two people are openly or silently at odds. But injustice loves company. Soon others are drawn into the web and two sides form. Eventually, the entire church or group disintegrates into factions.

In the Civil War, following the battle of Chancellorsville, the rear guard of Stuart's cavalry sounded the alarm that Union troops were attacking. The first and third Virginia regiments promptly charged each other, killing many. Like those troops, we sometimes forget who the enemy really is. We turn on our allies and begin lobbing shells into their camp. The worst wounds in the church community are self-inflicted.

What if you are attending a church deeply divided into factions? Maybe one group follows the founding pastor of your church who has recently retired. In their minds, no one can match his or her abilities and anointing. Maybe another faction has rallied around another in your church who has a gifted personality and magnetic charisma. This leader has such wisdom, eloquence, wit, and intellectual keenness. This person is dynamic and fantastic, but he or she is also the "enemy" to the faction following the founding pastor. And there's the rub.

Maybe you even have a third group—the conservative reactionaries or traditionalists. They are distressed that the church is letting down the old standard. They wonder if some of the new members are even truly Christians. They think the solution to everything is getting back to the old paths. Perhaps you even have a fourth group—a super-spiritual group who is wholly disgusted with these baby, weak Christians fussing and fighting with each other. This group considers itself above it all and whispers to each other, "Isn't it just terrible, the way they act?" They thank God that they are true followers of Christ and not mere humans.

Such factions may adopt leaders who are totally unaware that they are the "heroes" of said factions. Have you ever seen this kind of a divided church? What would (or should) you do if you ever become part of one? Get help! Once broken relationships have deteriorated into factions and discord, hope and help must come from outside the group. Factions won't settle their own disputes. There are too many people and interests involved. No settlement will satisfy everybody. Your only hope is to go outside your church. There you must get help. A divided church needs an outside authority. It should be someone all sides accept as spiritual and wise, and to whom all will submit their wills. Such a church needs an apostle, one with God's authority and wisdom. This kind of apostolic ministry may fall to a wise, old, spiritual monarch in the denomination, or it could be an elected official. Whoever it is, it must be a man or woman of wisdom and insight who is willing to get involved as a judge.

The church then submits itself to a sort of binding arbitration, with the outside authority sitting as judge. After hearing enough to discern the essence of the problem, he or she retires to seek God's wisdom. When the decision is rendered, it is final and all sides submit to it. Doesn't this plan make better sense than the alternatives? Isn't it better than letting strife destroy the church? Doesn't this plan make better sense than Christians dragging their complaints against each other into a secular court to be decided by a nonbeliever?

Is your church divided into factions? Rather than hoping someone in the church will emerge as the savior, seek an outside wise leader. Surrender the decision to him or her. Who knows? Picking such an arbitrator may be the first thing in years to which you can get everyone to agree.

what about you?

Can you think of someone somewhere whom you are holding something against? Or has God reminded you of someone who seems to be holding something against you? Have you thought of some third parties, several people who are breaking fellowship with each other? What should you do? If God is convicting you about any of these things, follow his advice and take action. Go to the one you may have hurt or to the one who hurt you. Get involved in helping others who seem to have an unraveling relationship. And if your whole church is in a mess, start campaigning to recruit a wise outside authority to help reconcile everyone.

Do you know of a broken relationship or a breaking one? Will you take the action necessary to sow the seeds of peacemaking?

If you do, you will reap a great and satisfying harvest of righteousness!

What are your specific plans to practice the discipline of peacemaking this week?

PART 4
discipline of response

In the discipline of response, we manage our responses to the experiences life brings us, both good and bad. Much—or perhaps *most*—of our spiritual growth comes as we learn to respond in a Christlike way to both difficulties and blessings. The disciplines of action, abstinence, and relationships are invaluable to our spiritual progress. But if we focus only on these, we will miss the most powerful discipline of all—the discipline of response to life. How we respond to our enemies, suffering, material blessings, and even marriage or divorce can advance or erode the gains we make from other spiritual disciplines. God is always forming us, not just when we are fasting or having devotions. God uses life itself as his formative tool. Our responses to searing criticism from coworkers can be the basis of our spiritual formation, like fasting or prayer can be. Of course, fasting and prayer help us know how to respond rightly, so we can't dismiss all the disciplines in this book and merely respond. A right response to life is not automatic. If anything, our natural responses are more often the wrong ones. Thus, it is a spiritual *discipline* to respond the way Christ calls us to respond.

22. response

Consider it pure joy, my brothers, whenever you face trials of many kinds, because you know that the testing of your faith develops perseverance. Perseverance must finish its work so that you may be mature and complete, not lacking anything.

—James 1:2–4

The spiritual discipline of response is managing our reactions to what life brings us—both good and bad. This concept is a novel one for a book on spiritual disciplines, yet the discipline of response is vital. Our characters are formed by the many tiny reactions we have to bad things like opposition, suffering, pain, temptation, divorce, enemies, defeat, persecution, the death of a loved one, and even our own impending deaths. Similarly, we are changed by how we respond to good things such as wealth, power, promotion, favor, opportunity, or success. We do not respond to these things in a single moment. Over time we make hundreds of little responses, and they come to form us spiritually. Practicing the disciplines of action, abstinence, and relationships helps us develop Christian responses, yet responding is a discipline in itself. It is more natural to respond to success by attributing it to our own cleverness than to give others the glory. Thus, it is a *discipline*. The response may be in what we say, how we act, or the attitudes we develop in our thoughts, but we are responding a thousand times every day. Each of our responses becomes a thread that weaves together the rope of our characters. Our characters are the totals of our choices. In the spiritual discipline of response, we braid into that rope Christlike responses to life's situations.

bad things and good people

Practicing the discipline of response develops the habit of using life experiences as a curriculum for spiritual growth. We learn to see both blessings and difficulties as the course outline for our spiritual development. Christians who take this approach are just as likely to be shocked at being diagnosed with cancer as anyone else. But Christians practicing this discipline soon begin to wonder how cancer can make them better people and even how it might help them serve others. They will fight the cancer and pray for healing, but simultaneously they will seek to respond to it in a Christlike manner. This is a hard assignment. It can't be done in a single response but must be accomplished on hundreds of occasions as new oncology reports come in and new procedures are tried. This is why it is a *discipline*; responding to life's experiences is repetitive and must become habitual in order to form us. Followers of God are not exempt from tragedy. We are, however, able to face difficulties differently. God does not reward his people for their obedience by doling out pleasant circumstances. Christians do not automatically get to skip the difficulties of life. Being a Christian is not about getting an exemption from evil; it is about having the resources to deal with evil when it comes our way.

God uses evil

We must be careful that we don't think God inflicts these evils upon us. It is a narrow ledge to walk: seeing evil as being *used* by God and avoiding seeing evil as being *caused* by him. God does not send cancer to us so we'll become better people. Cancer results from the fallen condition of our world, and God is at work on earth reversing the effects of the fall, including cancer. Eventually, he will triumph. For now, however, there is evil in the world, and God allows it. Because God could prevent evil from befalling us yet chooses not to, we know that evil is allowed to exist for some purpose. God did not prompt Joseph's brothers to sell him into slavery; Satan did. Yet while the brothers meant it for evil, God was able to use Joseph's situation for good. God can use evil circumstances to produce good results. This is why it is so important to have the right responses when bad things happen to us. When we experience evil, we ought to ask, "How can God use this?" but never say, "God did this to me." So what are some of the bad things that happen to people? What are some of the bad things that have happened to you? Can you see how God used those evils to accomplish something good in your life?

temptation

Are you facing temptation? What sort of temptation? Is the Devil hounding you so that you can find no relief? At every corner, do you face a new onslaught so powerful you can hardly resist? We can respond by surrendering to the Tempter who is weakening our wills, or we can resist temptation and strengthen our wills for future battles. God uses temptation to strengthen our wills. Every time we resist, we show our fidelity to God and make resistance in the future easier. Each successful resistance builds the muscles of our wills and strengthens our resolve to obey. It is up to us. Temptation brings the opportunity to either weaken or strengthen our wills. The Christian response to temptation is resistance.

opposition

Are you doing what you know to be the right thing but find someone opposing you? Have you been doing your best yet been told it isn't good enough? Perhaps there is a whole group of people opposed to you. They turn your successes into failures and your words into jokes. Perhaps no matter what we attempt, our opponents turn our accomplishments into dust. We can respond by simply giving up, or we can let God use these oppositions to develop perseverance in us. Without opposition, how can we develop determination? It is up to us. Opposition brings the opportunity to either develop perseverance or give up. The Christian response to opposition is to persevere.

enemies

Enemies are not only those who oppose us, but also those who are truly out to destroy us. Do you have an enemy? We can respond by fighting back and getting even, or we can let God use our enemies to develop love in us. Without enemies, how will we ever develop the kind of selfless love that Jesus had? Even non-Christians love their friends. Christians love their enemies—and even pray for them. Christians forgive their enemies before they've been asked to. It is up to us. Enemies bring opportunities to either fight back or love. The Christian response to our enemies is to love.

rejection

Did your father reject you? Or your mother? Did a friend or spouse walk away from you, discarding you like a piece of trash? Did a group of people reject you so that you still feel the sting? We can respond with anger, resentment, and self-deprecation, or we can let God use our rejection to develop a sweet spirit in us. How is it that the sweetest people often have experienced the most crushing blows? The crushing lets the sweet scent of Christ escape. Without rejection we are unlikely to develop this sweet spirit. It is up to us. Rejection brings the opportunity to express either sourness or sweetness. The Christian response to rejection is to identify with Christ's own rejection, allowing his character to be displayed.

division

Are you a part of a family or fellowship that seems hopelessly divided? Are your coworkers at odds and alienated from each other? We can respond by taking sides in the dispute, or God can use that division to help us learn to be a peacemaker. Without conflict we are unlikely to ever develop peacemaking skills. It is up to us. Division and strife bring the opportunity either to join in the fray or to learn to be a peacemaker. The Christian response to division is neither to join the battle nor to stand aloof, but to bring the sides together for reconciliation.

injustice

Are you a victim of injustice? Are you an injured party? We can respond by nursing injuries until they grow into a full-blown grudges and turn us into bitter people, or we can let God use those injustices to develop a forgiving spirit in our hearts. Without experiencing injustice, we are unlikely to learn forgiveness. It is up to us. Our injuries present a fork in the road— one path leading down the blind alley of bitterness, the other leading into the garden of grace and forgiveness. The Christian response to injustice is to forgive and let God collect on the debt of injustice.

suffering

Are you facing suffering? Is your mind constantly preoccupied with your pain? Do you wonder why others seem to have no pain and face no misery like yours? We can respond by doubting God's goodness and mercy, or we can develop a deeper faith in God and a greater willingness to trust him. Without suffering we will undoubtedly develop only a moderate trust in God. It is easier to believe that God is good when life is good. However, a Christian proclaims God's goodness when life is bad. It is up to us. Suffering brings the opportunity for either doubt or faith, either suspicion or trust. The Christian response to suffering is to develop increased faith in God and trust in his goodness.

failure

Have you failed miserably? Did you take a risk but it didn't pan out? Have you failed in business? Marriage? Life? Have you failed God? We can respond by giving up and running away, or we can let God use our failures to develop greater reliance on him. It is up to us. Without failure we are unlikely to develop full reliance on God. Instead, we will rely on ourselves. The Christian response to failure is greater trust in the Lord.

death

Are you facing death? Do you know that your exit from this life is looming? We can respond by surrendering to doubt and despair, or we can make our final days become the ultimate statement of faith. We can be either an example of doubt at death's door or an example of faith. Without facing death, we never know for certain the surety of our faith. It is up to us. Facing death is the final exam of faith. The Christian response to death is to recognize that it has no permanent sting—for we have eternal life.

tragedy

Have you lost a parent or spouse in a tragic accident? A son or daughter? Was it some tragedy you can't understand? Has life been unfair? Do you start each day mourning your loss? Is this tragedy your last thought at night as you drift off to sleep? Has your loss come to define who you are? We can respond with doubt and misgivings about God that may lead us eventually to reject him, or we can allow God to sooth the agony of tragedy in our lives, extracting from us tenderness toward others who are in pain. We develop tenderness for others as we process our own pain. It is up to us. Personal tragedy presents a choice either to head down the road of despair or to let God develop tenderness within us. The Christian response to tragedy is to let God create a tender spirit within us.

good things and good people

We tend to think of bad experiences as being more powerful in shaping us than good ones. At least we hear more testimonies about that sort of shaping. Yet our blessings offer an equal opportunity to respond in a way that forms us spiritually. In fact, without experiencing some blessings, we will never develop some Christlike qualities.

power

Do you have power over others? Are you in leadership? Do you teach and have the power of awarding grades? Are you a parent? We can respond by exercising our power like a despot, or we can temper our power with mercy. It is up to us. Unless we have power, we may never learn true meekness or exercise true mercy. It takes power to be meek or merciful. The Christian response to power is to learn mercy and meekness.

success

Do others consider you successful? Do you think so too? Do you have it made? We can respond by taking credit for our successes and assume that less-successful people are simply lazy, stupid, or unmotivated, or we can use success as an opportunity to learn humility and gratefulness. The blessing of success can teach us how to be humble, giving others credit for their part in our victories. Success also presents an opportunity to become prideful, taking all credit for ourselves. It is up to us. Success can make us arrogant, self-reliant people who judge everyone else as deficient, or it can make us more humble and grateful people. The Christian response to success is to be humble, grateful, and compassionate.

supernatural touch

Have you had a miraculous spiritual experience from God? Has he healed you, given you impressive spiritual gifts, or delivered you from some bondage? We can respond with spiritual pride and condemnation toward those who are so spiritually deficient that they have not reached the level of spirituality we have, or we can give credit to God alone for our spiritual condition and humbly treat others with dignity and respect. It is up to us. The Christian response to God's supernatural touch is to give him the credit for the spiritual life he has blessed us with.

wealth

Are you rich? Certainly there are others who are richer than you, but how many people are poorer? Does your annual income place you in the top 20 percent of the world's people? We can respond by hoarding our treasures, constantly investing them to build "bigger barns" for ourselves, or we can open our hands and let our blessings of wealth serve others. It is up to us. The Christian response to wealth is to use it to the benefit of others.

health

Are you healthy? Sickness and suffering can be a means of growth if we respond to them properly, but so can health. We can respond by never valuing our health until we lose it, or we can learn to daily express gratitude to God for the vigor of our lives. It is up to us. The Christian response to health is to thank God for however we feel every day.

the all-day discipline

Many of the disciplines of action, abstinence, and relationships can be practiced at a set time. The discipline of response, however, must be practiced all day long. Wrong or right attitudes are not developed in an instant; they are the products of our consistent thought patterns repeated over days, weeks, and even years. Preventing wrong attitudes from developing takes a repeated discipline of laying down tracks for right thought patterns. The discipline of response requires constant, daily, and momentary effort. By learning to discipline our responses to what life brings us—both good and bad—we are trained to react as Christ would and are formed into his image.

how to begin practicing response

define your bad experiences

What bad situation do you now face? Identify it, even if it only seems like a little thing compared to the issues above. Ask yourself, "If God uses bad things in my life to make me better, what are those bad things?" Most Christians can think of at least one item in their lives that is painful, difficult, or at least irritating.

define your blessings

What blessings and opportunities have you received? What are the good things in your life that also require a right response if you are to become more Christlike?

describe the choice

When encountering any difficulty or blessing, you face a choice. Describe this choice, this fork in the road, and the two possible responses, one leading away from Christ and the other toward him.

determine to choose right

Decide that you *will* make the right choice in the many individual responses to your difficulties and blessings. All these little decisions make you who you are. But the big, initial decision gets you started on the path to using life's good and bad things to make you better.

discover accountability

The discipline of response is not a one-time event. It is an ongoing discipline. Find someone to check up on you frequently and monitor your success in learning to see both blessings and difficulties as a means of grace.

what about you?

What are your specific plans to practice the discipline of response this week?

What do you believe?

Many Christians today cannot fully answer this question. *Common Ground* by Keith Drury uses the Apostle's Creed as its guide to beautifully describe the core beliefs that all Christians at all times and everywhere have believed in—God as Creator and loving Father, the virgin birth and divinity of Jesus, Jesus' death and resurrection, the Holy Spirit, the church, the second coming, final judgment, and eternal life.

ISBN: 978-0-89827-354-0

wesleyan
publishing
house
www.wesleyan.org/wph
1.800.493.7539

God has more for you than what you're experiencing!

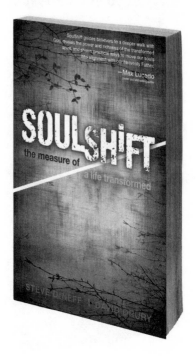

Now that you've learned about spiritual disciplines, experience transformational living through *SoulShift*.

Read a FREE excerpt and testimonials at www.WPHonline.com.

You can lead your entire church through the eight-week SoulShift journey with the SoulShift Family Ministry Kit, which includes both SoulShift for Children and Youth Kit and SoulShift Church Resource Kit.

SoulShift
9780898276978

Family Ministry Kit
9780898277203